TA'WIL AL-AHĀDITH

SHAH WALIYULLAH'S

TA'WIL AL-AHADITH

Rendered into English

by

G. N. JALBANI
Formerly Professor of Arabic
University of Sind

KITAB BHAVAN
New Delhi-1 10002

KITAB BHAVAN
Publishers, Distributors, Exporters & Importers
1784, Kalan Mahal, Darya Ganj,
New Delhi - 1100 02 (India)

Phones	:	(91-11) 23277392/93, 23274686, 32906494
Fax	:	(91-11) 23263383
Website	:	www.nusratalinasri.com
	:	www.kitabbhavan.com
Email	:	nasri@vsnl.com
	:	nusrat@bol.net.in

1st Published in India : 1981
4th Edition : 2011

ISBN : 81-7151-046-9

Book Code : T00005

Printed & Published in India by :
Nusrat Ali Nasri for KITAB BHAVAN
1784, Kalan Mahal, Darya Ganj,
New Delhi - 1100 02 [India]

PREFACE

Ta'wil al-Aḥādīth is one of the most important works of Shāh Walīyullāh of Delhi. On a subject like this, it is indeed a unique presentation. Brevity and employment of a particular terminology are the main features of its style.

This small treatise deals with the interpretation of the stories and the explanation of the major events which had taken place during the days of those prophets whose names have come down in the Holy Qur'ān. For every event a natural cause has been ciṭed, as nothing happens in the world without a cause. Even miracles have their causes. But, if it is necessary to create a thing, God creates it even if there be no causes, as He possesses infinite knowledge. These causes, however, are known to him who has thoroughly comprehended the science of the working system of the whole universe and has properly understood both the earthly and the heavenly causes working in it. Shāh Ṣāḥib undoubtedly possessed a copious share of that science. A hint towards that is given in the end on the topic "Wonders of the World".

This book has been so named, as all the happenings which happen in the world are like a dream and a vision, and they first appear in the Similitudinary World (*'Ālam-ul-Mithāl*) in a suitable form. Some persons who are spiritually advanced come to know of them in their dreams. An example of it is found in the chapter named "Joseph" in the Holy Qur'ān. The dream of seven cows seen by the king of Egypt was correctly interpreted by the Prophet Joseph. Shāh Ṣāḥib himself has explained somewhere the reason of his giving such a name to the book. According to him, for every change which is to ṭake place, there ought to be a required capability both in the prophet of that age and in the people to whom he is being sent.[1]

1. *Al-Fauz al-Kabir fi Uṣūl al-Tafsir*, p. 402 :
و مراد از تاویل آلست که قصهٔ که واقع شد آن را مبدأ می باشد از
استعداد پیغامبر و قوم او از تدبیری که خدائی تعالیٰ در آن وقت خواسته
است -

In this work, the history of the evolution of the human mind is traced, and for all the important events, including the miracles, their natural causes have been mentioned. It bears some resemblance to the *Fuṣū ul-Ḥikam* of Ibn-ul-'Arabī. Shāh Walīyullāh had studied *Fuṣūṣ* under the guidance of his father; thus, there is reason to believe that he had been influenced by the work of al Shaikh al-Akbar, but the Shaikh has not explained, as Shāh Sāhib has done, the secrets underlying the important events which had taken place in the days of the prophets.

The book was first translated by the present translator into the Sindhī language and was published by the Shāh Walīyullāh Academy, Hyderabad, in 1964. Looking to the usefulness and importance of the book, its English rendering was considered necessary. This book, it is hoped, will appeal to the modern mind and will be found to its temper and taste. The narration throughout is interesting and appealing. It is, therefore, that Shāh Walīyullāh has rightly claimed to have come for the scientific age, wherein people were not prepared to accept everything blindly.

G. N. JALBANI

CONTENTS

THANKSGIVING

In the Name of God, the Beneficent, the Merciful

All praise be to God, Who sent the prophets with His clear command and guidance. He placed the treasures of knowledge of His person (*dhāt*), of His names and of the secrets of His creation in their hearts. He made their tongues to speak that by which he whose nature (*fiṭrah*) is free from defect can be reformed and improved, and in order that an argument can be established against him who persists in his obstinacy in denying and rejecting the truth.

He, then, moved their lives towards the multifarious stages of His nearness, and by His power and prowess showed to them the rare events. Many blessings descended on them when they were enshrowded by His mercy and help. He lightened their hardships when they smote and hit them repeatedly with a view to keeping their hearts steady and unshakable.

Many miracles appeared at their hands, so that he who perishes by a clear sign may perish because of his wretchedness, and he who lives by a clear sign may live on account of his good fortune.[1] At the time of His suppressing and waging war against infidelity, He turned upside down many plans of the enemies and threw them back on their faces. Many enemies were finished and sent to their graves by the accepted prayers of the prophets. They had seen many a dream in which the secrets of the Intermediary World and those of the Day of Resurrection and all that was to come upon man in his future life were disclosed to them. Many events were shown to them in which the secrets of the Angelic World and those of the World of Divinity were represented before them in suitable forms by which they came to know of the meaning implied in them.

He has placed a secret in each one of those events which can

1. Qur'ān, viii. 42.

be understood only by those whom He has chosen and whom He has taught the science of the interpretation of dreams (*Ta'wīl al-Aḥādīth*), and by those whose hearts He had expanded with both the acquired and the hereditary knowledge.

Glory be to Him Who gives from His knowledge and provision whomsoever He likes. I bear witness that there is no god but Allah, Who is alone without any partner, a witness which may fulfil the right God has on His servants. And I bear witness that our Chief, Muḥammad, is His servant and His messenger, and is one under whose banner Adam and others will stand for protection on the Day of Judgment, when the situation will be too grave and serious.

After this, the weak servant, needy of the mercy of his generous Lord, namely Aḥmad, known as Walīyullāh b. 'Abd-ur-Raḥīm, says that these narrations are the springs which have gushed out of the science of the "Interpretation of Dreams" and are the branches which have shot out of the great, lofty tree of the secret of heritage.[2]

I have named this treatise as *Ta'wīl al-Aḥādīth*, so that this heading may lift the thick veil which has covered the real truth. All, abundant, excellent, limitless and countless praise be to God.

2. Here is a reference to Shāh Ṣāhib's having inherited this branch of science from his forefathers.

INTRODUCTION

Know that when God sends down a Divine science to human beings through the tongue of a human being, coming down from the Original Source (God) in the form of an emanation towards them, the way which it follows is not that of a metaphor or an allusion just as it happens in the sciences of the common people; but its way towards it is that of *al-Tajawwuz al-Ṭabī'ī* For example, when the knowledge of a certain condition which is to happen to a man is poured into his senses, it (knowledge) is represented to him in the form of a dream made of both the voluntary and involuntary actions of the bodies and the animals bearing resemblance in some way to that poured out general condition.

There is a man in whom the knowledge is poured that he would soon become a king; he dreams (the symbols of) kingship in the form of a crown or an elephant, and then he sees that someone comes to him and puts a crown on his head or makes him ride an elephant. The interpreter on hearing it (the dream) says that this dream signifies that the dreamer will acquire kingship. By the crown and the elephant is meant the conferment of kingship, while the coming of a man and his putting the crown on his head and making him ride the elephant is a cause of the affair. It is so because man by his nature is disposed to think that there is a cause for every happening; thus unavoidably that cause assumes before him in this dream the form of someone who comes and participates in putting the crown on his head.

Similarly, when God intends to draw man's attention towards a general reality, the nature (*ṭaur*) of which transcends the nature of senses, then He draws his attention towards it through a story or a speech, the sum and substance of which happens to imitate His intention, as the dream imitates the desired event. In this respect, by the show of dignity of the kings and the execution of their order in the country when seen in the dream is meant the exaltation and the greatness of God. To that refers the Word of God: "Nay, He, both His hands are spread out."[1] Similarly, there are other allegories, such as laughing, etc.

Accordingly, when God intended to inform us of His being Generous, He looked at the form of generosity it had in the dream, and that was the spreading of the hands. He, therefore, spoke to us about it in that way. And when He intended to inform us of His being the Administrator (*mudabbir*) of the heavens and the earth, He looked at the form of administration it had in the dream, and it was the dignity of the kings in the position of their authority. Thus, He spoke to us about it in that manner. However, the foundation of His speech, if you were to thoroughly examine certain forms, is not based on the relations mentioned in the explanatory science (*'Ilm al-Bayān*).

By *al-Tajawwuz al-Ṭabī'ī* I mean the imitation of an orderly happening and an event or of a speech implied in an allusion, through a general secret hinting at the connections which the nature (*ṭabī'ah*) takes consideration of in the dream, when it receives the general knowledge and forms a picture of it.

Know that the conditions which are to happen to the perfect men unexpectedly and the orderly events seen in the dream signify the consummation of their desires, the reason being that the predication (*ḥukm*) of the conditions and events is like the predication of the dream. Similarly, all the events which take place in the world are dreams, and they, however, have certain principles and forms. Some of the principles are as follows:

(1) The intention of God about His servants, namely, to effect administration among them through inspirations (*ilhāmāt*), transformations (*iḥālāt*) and the raising of causes (*taqrībāt*). Thus, Divine Mercy (*Raḥmūt*) personally turns towards the establishment of the best order (*niẓām khair*) and naturally moves towards finding out an event. He, then, in order to bring about that event, gives rise to an inspiration or to a transformation or to a cause among His servants, and then, according to the usual course, selects the nearest of the things (sufficient to bring about that event) avail-

1. Qur'ān, v. 64.

able on that day. Consequently, an external event gradually appears through the appearance of the cause and the inspiration, and then the natures as well as the minds (*nufūs*) accept that event according to their capability. Now, here, that event is only a form and a dream, while that administration put into effect is a principle and an interpretation. An example of it is as follows: When God intended to appoint a vicegerent in the earth, He created Adam. Adam was then encompassed by a similitudinary reality by which is meant the Paradise. As such, he was dealt with as the inmates of the Paradise are dealt with, and the door of his becoming the vicegerent in the earth became closed.[2] Thereafter, some causes appeared which, according to the purity of his heart, gave him a warning to the effect that his eating the tree is forbidden for him, as this would lead him to his removal from the Paradise. This warning then became a necessary revelation for him. The Satan, who was essentially mischievous, was well prepared to prompt evil thoughts into his mind. The nature of Adam again was disposed to the eating of the tree with the result that he ate it and, in consequence, was blamed and turned out. All this was a dream and a vision, the interpretation of which is as follows: God's intention in creating Adam was that he should become a vicegerent in the earth and attain his specific perfection (*kamāl nau'ī*). As regards his being prohibited from eating the tree, the prompting by Satan of evil thoughts, his being reprimanded and, finally, his expulsion from the Paradise, all this was a form of the cause according to his coming out gradually from the world of similitude to the world of mortals.

(2) At times, a certain person by his very nature happens to be prepared for perfection, such as his taking notice of a Divine secret or keeping a continuous connection with the Sublime Assembly (*Mala'-i-A'lā*) or getting dyed with a Divine dye. He acquires this according to his attainment of maturity. The appear-

2 Adam, even though he was an earthly person, yet because of his perfection he had acquired an other-worldly body, and, thus, was lodged in the Paradise. At that time, his body looked like a similitudinary body (*Tafhimat*, Vol. II, p. 118). From this it also appears that it was an earthly Paradise where Adam was deluded by the Satan.

ance of his perfection, however, goes by a known order (*niẓām*), when he gets some freedom from the veils of nature (*ṭabī'ah*), of custom and of the body. Sometimes, when he gains such freedom from these veils, this connection (with the Sublime Assembly), this dye and these moments of freedom assume in his senses or in his dream the form of a regular event. An interpretation of it is one of those things (namely, Divine secret, connection with the Sublime Assembly and getting dyed with a Divine dye). An example of it is as follows: The Holy Prophet, in the very beginning of his nature, was found connected with the World of Divinity, bearing resemblance to the Sublime Assembly and was free from every kind of impurity. As such, his nature began perfecting time after time. At times, his perfection appeared in the form of the splitting of the chest. At times, it appeared in the shape of the speech of the angel Gabriel while he (Gabriel) was sitting between the heaven and the earth. And at times, he was weighed with the rest of the people and outweighed them all, and at times, in the form of the Ascension (*Mi'rāj*).

Similarly, the Prophet Abraham (Ibrāhīm) was strong-hearted in following the law of Nature. When his nature became perfect, it appeared in the form of a happening, and it was his look upon the stars, the moon and the sun. By their setting he made an inference that they were not those who had created him. Don't you see the jealous: how his jealousy appears during a particular happening? The nature, therefore, is a principle and the happening is a form.

(3) The language of the Real (*al-Ḥaqq*) differs according to the capability of the person addressed with the result that, at times, he hears a particular language and, at times, an ordinary one. The Divine Mercy (*Raḥmūt*) also, at times, intends one state and, at times, some other state. Thus, the hearer, at times, happens to be dyed with this state and, at times, with that state, and in every state he receives what suits him best. Then, for this secret and for man's coming out from power to action, an event is formed, such as a command, a prohibition, a punishment, a reprehension, an abrogation, a ransoming and a forgiveness. An example of it is as follows: In the beginning, fifty prayers were prescribed on the occasion of the Ascension. In the end, God said :

"The word does not change before Me."[3] These are five and these are fifty. These are fifty by language expressive of permissible liberty (*lisān tajawwuz*), and five by language expressive of reality. The object in both the cases is one and the same, but God, on account of some wisdom He had in mind, concealed the reality in the beginning.

The Prophet Jonah (Yūnus) had firmly decided upon destroying his people, while the Divine Curse had not yet reached its stage and assumed an ugly aspect. But when he turned to God and conversed with Him secretly, he took notice of that aspect. It is just like this. Someone sees a dream in which an address is represented to him in the form of a story pointing out to the rottenness of fruits and the breaking of the vessels. When he wakes up from sleep he understands that the object behind it was to draw his attention to that aspect (namely, the deterioration of his condition). To illustrate further, a person of phlegmatic nature finds in his sleep that he is caught in by cold, is drowned in the ocean or is smitten by snow and rain. Similarly, he who is overcome by the faculty of anger sees in his dream, when that faculty comes in a clash with his angelic faculty, that, as if, a lion is attacking him. All these things are pointing to the aspects of his mind, firmly established in it in a form that resembles the natural story. Jonah was addressed through such a story, so that it may serve as an example for him, not that it should become a general rule.

Know that when God desires to manifest an extraordinary work (*khāriq 'ādah*) in order to effect administration, He does so in the form of an ordinary course, however weak that ordinary course may be. For example, a man suffers from a minor illness, and when a physician sees him, he does not pay any attention to him, as he never thinks that he would die of this illness, but the decree of God appears even in that minor illness and he dies.

Thus, there are weak causes for the extraordinary works as well, which are, as if, in accompaniment of the execution of the decree of God and His Providence towards the earthly causes, so that the order (*'ādah*) should not be completely broken. There

3. Qur'ān, l. 29.

are hints both in the Qur'ān and in the Tradition which give an indication of such causes. In the story, however, there is a hint and a meaning, which a gnostic understands, nay, every righteous and intelligent person can also comprehend it. The Holy Prophet has said: "When God decides for man that he should die at a certain place, He fixes for him a need to go to that place." Thus, giving rise to his need is just to take into consideration the course of voluntary acts, so that the order may not break.

God willing, we are soon to point out the interpretation of every happening and the reason of the particular form it takes, and are also to point out those weak causes behind every extraordinary work. You, therefore, wait for our hints and watch with vigilance when we narrate the story.

ADAM AND ENOCH

The faculties of the spirits of the heavenly bodies gathered in some corner of the earth, and the origin of the species of man (humanity) pleaded to God for its appearance in the world of mortals (material world). Consequently, elements became balanced and turned into a fine putrefaction. Then, God, according to those conditions, decided to create His vicegerent in the earth, that is, someone in whom there may be an ample scope for progress and for the acquisition of the perfect moral character. He may combine both the angelic and the bestial faculties which give rise to the emergence of the Divine states, like goodness and love. He may also be worthy to receive a Law (*Sharī'ah*) from above, till he may become the universe itself, a copy of the Divine Mercy (*Raḥmūt*) which encompasses all the realities of the universe in general.

There were, however, angels who deserved to be inspired with the knowledge of the future. They were made of elements and were the officers working in elements under inspiration from God. They received an inspiration that God is soon to create a vicegerent whose business would be such and such. He will shed blood and make mischief in the earth, and will, in consequence, be punished both in this world and in the hereafter. But the wisdom implied in his creation did not become clear to them, because they knew only what they were inspired with. Thus, according to the condition of those angels, the wisdom of God and His Providence desired to let them know what they knew not.

Firstly, they were told through general inspiration (*ilhām ijmālī*) that God possesses wisdom which they do not know; secondly, through an explanatory event, which would be a commentary and an elucidation of that wisdom. Then, with the command of God and His intention, a balanced matter became collected, which was, as if, a combination of all the different parts of the earth. When any temperate object is touched by something hot, it becomes hot, and becomes cold when touched by something cold. Thus, that matter on account of the adjacent power combined all the parts of the earth and was, as if, their leaven. At that time it became like a putrefacted matter which gives rise to the creation of worms, save that its putrefaction was spiritual and not unclean, because it received a stroke from a strong spiritual faculty. It was just like the putrefaction of the seminal fluid in the belly of a woman which, when God breathes the spirit into it, becomes alive.[1]

In short, when the intention by Adam's creation was the creation of the species, its predication so penetrated his individuality that he looked as if he was the species itself; and the awareness of this secret also penetrated the very essence of his individuality. Besides, when he was the result of the combined concentrations of the spiritualities, their predication also penetrated his soul (*Rūḥ*).

As his acquaintance with his Lord was new, and the system of the elements and the humours had not become strong in him as yet, he was, for some time, dealt with as the inmates of the Paradise were dealt with. Thereafter, a cause took place, so that he may exclusively devote himself to the purpose he was created for, and that the predications of his natural disposition may dominate him.

A spirituality suitable to the angels was implanted in him, and he, on that account, deserved to receive the inspiration. A bestial spirituality was also infixed in him, by which he deserved to be a vehicle for the ugly states arising out of the abundance of food. When both the angelic and the bestial faculties united he gained an intellect more perfect than all the other intellects of the animals. His intellect then penetrated his lust, his anger and his needs. Thereafter, he was inspired with the wonderful necessary works of life and also with the ways of finding out different kinds of arts and crafts. His intellect penetrated his angelic state as

1. Here Shāh Walīyullāh seems to have been influenced by the philosophical romance, *Ḥayy Ibn Yaqẓān* (the living one son of the waking one) of Ibn Ṭufail.

well, and he was, thus, inspired with the various forms of worship and purification. God then established wonderful laws for all those matters for his children. According to these three principles, some happenings had happened to him, and they are as follows:

(1) The elemental angels and the angels employed as officers to look after the affairs of people were commanded to prostrate before Adam in person, while the angels of the Sublime Assembly were commanded to prostrate before him in form (*ashbāh*) with the result that they all appeared in the form of prostration-makers, just as the angel Gabriel, while inquiring about "Faith," "Islam" and "Goodness," had appeared (before the Holy Prophet) in the form of a bedouin Arab. It is, therefore, that the Holy Prophet had said: "Gabriel had come to you to teach your religion to you." In the light of this explanation, all the angels prostrated before him.

In short, their prostration implied a deep secret, and that deep secret was that they were worshipping God alone in all that they were doing for the children of Adam, namely, praying for them and discussing among themselves about them. Thus, Adam and his children were a direction for their worship. This secret, then, assumed the form of an event and became a revelation making it necessary for them to prostrate.

There was, however, Satan among them, who by his very nature was disposed to envy, grudge and haughtiness, but he did not have an opportunity to manifest those evils. By his very nature he was completely given over to wickedness and mischief, but as the influence of the angels had dominated him for some time, he had entered into their fold. When he was commanded to prostrate, he disobeyed God. He, therefore, cursed him very severely with the result that he was encompassed by sins and became, as if, changed into a different form and exclusively applied to wickedness.[2]

2. As Satan was a personification of wickedness and mischief, he must have played a terrible mishchief with Adam. The way Shāh Ṣāḥib has given the description of Satan lends support to the interpretation made by Maulānā 'Ubaidullāh Sindhī in his *Ilhām ar-Rahmān* on pp. 94-5, that Satan had brought a female jinn and had actually done the act of sexual intercourse before him, inciting him thereby to do the same, as that all, he told him, would be the cause of his eternal life in Paradise.

(2) Adam was encompassed by the faculties of the spirits and imaginations of the Sublime Assembly. The imagination of the Throne had also turned towards him, with the result that he became (an inmate) in Paradise, while as a matter of fact he was still in his place on the earth. In consequence, the rules of Paradise were applied to him. But as there was a sensual urge in him, he very eagerly longed for a female of his own genus, and strongly imagined her form with the result that she appeared out of his imagination.

Thereafter, God created a cause, so that Adam may devote himself exclusively to the purpose He had created him for. He also commanded his sensual and greedy nature to obey the inspiration it may receive from the source of wickedness, which it obeyed. But there Adam felt some doubt and found the true knowledge mixed up with the false one, and also felt some sort of hardness in his heart which somehow prevented him from perceiving that truth as it actually was.

Forbidden Tree

The truth is that Adam, prior to his being in the Paradise, was commanded by the tongue of Providence, peculiar to that occasion, that the eating of the tree was forbidden for him which, if eaten, would lead to his expulsion from the Paradise and land him in trouble, hunger and thirst. He was also inspired with the true knowledge that his eating of it would be the cause of his eternity, i.e. the survival of the (human) species, the appearance of the command of God and His intention. Both the command and the inspiration descended on his nature, and here the affair became dubious to him. He became perplexed and hesitant and could not understand what he should do. God alluded his perplexity and hesitation to forgetfulness (*nisyān*).

Then the sensual urge in his breast got excited with the result that he ate of the tree.[3] This, as a matter of fact, was the result of the true knowledge having mixed up with the false one. It was

3. From here it could be safely made out that by eating of the tree was meant the sexual intercourse, as this is the only food of the sensual urge when it is excited. The late Maulānā 'Ubaidullāh Sindhī in his *Ilhām ar-Raḥmān*, pp. 94-5, has also given the same interpretation.

also the result of the hardness of his heart and the absence of the proper appearance of the inspiration. He, therefore, thought that perhaps the meaning of eternity was his survival in Paradise. Thus, this knowledge being mixed up with falsehood was a Satanic prompting of an evil thought.

It was indeed a cause for the intention of God which He had made in the eternity. As a result of that (eating of the tree), the predications (*aḥkām*) of nature (*ṭabī'ah*) appeared in him and the order (*niẓām*) of the elements and the humours prevailed upon him. Paradise was lost, the angelic providence remained concealed from him and the natural providence made its full appearance. He was then told that when the nature (*ṭabī'ah*) will smite his children and they would not be fit to receive the true inspiration, it would become necessary in the generosity and the wisdom of God to send messengers to them from among them. Those who will follow the guidance, there will be no fear on them, nor will they grieve, and he who will reject it will enter the Hell-fire, and after that he will be condemned very strongly.

The secret of all this was that there was a conflict between the angelic soul and the nature (*ṭabī'ah*). The latter had encompassed the former from every side. He then importunately pleaded to God for protection and was, in consequence, guided towards the spiritual predication in nature. He thereby fulfilled the predication of both the nature and the soul. His case at that time was like that of a mystic (*sālik*) who had devoted himself exclusively to God and had gone on ascending and then finally returned with God to journey in the world (*khalq*). This return of his from a high state to a low one was, in a way, his descent (*hubūṭ*).[4]

(3) When his soul became free from the veils of nature (*ṭabī'ah*) he was inspired with the knowledge of the useful works of life (*irtifāqāt*) and the needs the human beings will feel in the future. He was also inspired with the knowledge of the tools, by the help of which he could make progress, and the knowledge of the scansion of voices and that of the way he may utter word in front of

4. According to Shāh Ṣāḥib, the word *hubūṭ* here means the descent of the state, from the higher to the lower, and not of the place.

everything. There, however, he found, that his reality was paying attention to everything.

God then manifested those things in the Similitudinary World as Adam had known them in his imagination. He, then, asked the angels about them and their names and the ways the useful work (*irtifāq*) could be done. But they had no knowledge of that, as no such clear reason to understand them was placed in their nature which should have penetrated senuality, anger and the needs. Thus, the wisdom of God appeared, and His favour on the angels, in teaching them what they knew not, became complete.

(4) One day when he (Adam) was intellectually applied, he came to know that he is the origin of the human beings, and their becoming good and bad would be determined according to the difference of their capabilities (*isti'dādāt*). Then, their forms were caused to appear in the Similitudinary World by way of complection for Adam and an explanation of the decision taken for their existence in that World (of Similitudes). God, then, asked them: "Am I not your Lord?" They replied "Yes." This reply of theirs was, however, made by the tongue of nature (*fiṭrah*) prior to its mixture with the constitution (*ṭabī'ah*), which (mixture) was likely to cause an impediment in the expression. Thus, they on that account were taken to task, as that event was an explanation of the origin of their nature. That event was the form of nature, just as a thing is represented by its form in the dream. The punishment was then attributed to it (that nature) both in the Divine sciences which descend upon the perceptive faculties of the Sublime Assembly and those of the human beings.

(5) He was inspired with the doing of some work of the first stage of the socio-economics (*al-Irtifāq al-Awwal*) Consequently, he took to cultivation, harvesting, treading the corn, subjugating the animals and cooking the food. He also invented some languages and found guidance to the styles of speech, etc. He took care of the affairs of progeny and established rules for worship.

The Prophet Enoch (Idrīs), in the beginning of his life, was a partisan of Adam and followed his footsteps in the natural, God-given human sciences. His perfection in those days was implied in his devotion to acquiring the attributes (*aḥkām*) of the human form. Rising from this stage he turned to acquire the wisdom implied in *insilākh*[5] (jumping out of humanness into angelicness).

He, then, applied himself exclusively to the acquisition of the attributes of the Self-unfolding Existence (*al-Wujūd al-Munbasiṭ*) which is after the form of the universe (existing things), and moved further to the point of the Divine Aspect (*Lāhūt*). After that, he descended towards the sciences of nature (*ṭabī'iyāt*), divinity, astronomy, medicine and socio-economics. It was so because he was a handicraftsman, strong in his intellect and imagination. As a result of it, many sciences appeared from him, and the Divine Providence penetrated them and made them effective. Thus, they remained well preserved in spite of the change of generations and times. When one generation was wiped out, another came in its place, and when one age changed, the other one took its place. He was subsequently blessed in those sciences.

Then, the Magian and the Ḥanafī creeds sprang up. The sciences of medicine, of invocation (for God's help) and of astronomy became systematised and properly arranged. These sciences were true in those days, though the truth was mixed up with falsehood and the established reality was blended with the altered one.[6]

He, then, made still further progress and applied himself to the acquisition of the angelic aspect by restraining his nature (*ṭabī'ah*) and by stripping it off its requirements. Consequently, he was encompassed by the Heavenly state (Paradise) and was raised to a high station.

5. *Insilākh* means that the Latent Reality may force the Rational Soul (*Nafs Nāṭiqah*) to copy its representations to an extent it (Rational Soul) is reduced to nothingness. See *al-Khair al-Kathir*, p. 59.

6. The science of *da'wāt* is a system of incantation, held lawful by the orthodox Muslims, so long as man does not associate anything with God.

NOAH

He, in general, was so strong in the bestial faculty that it had become a veil over the face of his soul, preventing it from its attaining its perfection. Same was the case with the majority of people to whom he was sent. Accordingly, a Law (*Sharī'ah*) was prescribed for them under which they were obliged to pray and fast continuously and to do such acts of obedience as were to suppress this bestial faculty and awaken it towards humanity. They (the people of Noah), however, could not understand much the subtleties of the domestic and the acquired philosophy on account of their inclination to bestiality. As such, no abstruse sciences about these matters were revealed to them. Noah himself was calm in applying his imagination and thought towards knowing these subtle problems, and, thus, did not rise to the sciences of the Prophet Enoch (Idrīs) altogether.

His people were transgressors and unbelievers. They had spoiled the works of socio-economic development with the result that their road to God was closed. They had gone out of humanity even though, in form, they looked like human beings. In consequence, the Sublime Assembly became angry with them. When God looked at them, He cursed them and grew wrathful. Then a decision to destroy them was taken; however, it became necessary in the wisdom of God to give them a warning and the direction to the Truth first. It is so, because God has various tongues and many providences. If He becomes angry with a people by one tongue, He does not give up His kindness towards them by the other one.

Now, when the destruction of all the species and their recreation afresh was a great evil which God did not like, and when the heavenly and the earthly causes had not united together and assumed a modest aspect opposing the Divine Providence, it became necessary in His Providence to raise a cause for the preservation of the origins of the species. Noah was, thus, inspired with the preparation of a boat and for placing therein both males and females of all the kinds of species and also the seed of every tree which was not growing by itself. This is how God accomplished His affair.

The Divine Administration (*al-Tadbīr al-Ilāhī*) then waited for a great atmospheric change in order to punish them with it. When both the heavenly and the earthly causes agreed upon a universal deluge, God carried His decision through. It is seldom that a great change takes place, and it takes place only when many providences require and press for, as the providence of the earthly natures (*ṭabā'i'*), the providence of the heavenly orders (*aḥkām*) and the providence of the Divine arguments and also those of the Divine Laws (*Nawāmīs*) which have been prescribed for the people. But he who is given only a portion of the knowledge of one of these providences, and is unaware of the rest, accuses him of lying who attributes those changes to those causes. However, a complete and thorough knowledge combines all of them together.

All the sciences and affairs of the people of Noah were the result of these providences. It is for this reason that God made him as the second Adam. He was the first among the prophets who were raised to serve the Divine Providence, namely, to warn people, command them to obey the Law, dispute with the unbelievers and devise such ways and means as the Divine Providence requires. In all these matters, the way followed by the prophets comes to an end with him. His community was the first community raised for the people (to guide them).

When he was inspired with a certain device for the preservation of the human beings, there was implied in that inspiration some knowledge of the works of socio-economics, for which he commanded his children. Besides, that inspiration implied some knowledge of the trials, and he, therefore, cautioned his people against the Antichrist. In addition to these, that inspiration also implied some knowledge of the unity of God (*Tawḥīd*), the worship and the way of compelling the bestial nature to obey the order of the angelic one.

ABRAHAM

The sum and substance of his life-account is that he was very strongly inclined towards the requirements of Nature (*Fiṭrah*). The reason is that human beings differ in the manifestation of their moral character. There is one, for example, in whom bravery is found wanting, and there is another in whom it is present but is rather weak, and even with very hard bodily exercise it emerges but little not worth consideration. In some persons, it is in moderate form which does not appear, but only when invited towards that and does not become strong but only by the practice of suitable words and deeds and by participation in such actions in which there are possible indications of its (bravery's) appearance.

There is a person in whom bravery is strong. If he is restrained from the requirements of bravery, such as embarkation upon dangers, and is prevented from doing such works in which he has to demonstrate the feats of bravery, he could be restrained but with difficulty, and that restraining also would be very hard for him. In spite of that, however, he cannot remain free from the thoughts of bravery. And when he rushes into the deeds of bravery or is ordinarily invited towards them, he gets attracted towards them like sulphur which takes no time in burning when it catches fire.

There is again a person in whom bravery is found in extraordinarily strong form, to an extent that he cannot help meeting its requirements, nay, he is by necessity disposed towards them (requirements). If someone invites him to oppose them (requirements of bravery) he will never listen to the inviter, and no thought of cowardliness will ever occur to his mind. Now, this last person is the leader in bravery, who does not stand in need of any other leader in this respect. It then becomes the duty of the people who are comparatively of lower rank to hold fast to the result that he was overwhelmed by a state between death and life, like one which had once overwhelmed the Companions of the Cave (*Aṣḥāb al-Kahf*). He was then sent to them in that condition.

Every evil is represented by the form of an animal in the World of Divinity, according to its (evil's) natural relation with the animals. But the last evil will, however, assume the form of a man and then a universal destruction will draw near. Their evil, by the prayer of Ṣāliḥ, appeared in the form of a she camel, but when they killed it, that evil turned into a spirit and the punishment (*ṭūfān*) followed. Similarly, when the Antichrist will be killed, the evil will turn into a spirit and the great Resurrection (*Qiyāmah*) will take place. Punishment is the destruction of a certain people, but the Resurrection will be the destruction of all.

HEBER AND ṢĀLIḤ

Know that the case of both Heber (Hūd) and Ṣāliḥ, the case of their people who were lost in infidelity and transgression, the case of the Sublime Assembly in their having become angry with them, the decision of their (of the people of Heber and Ṣāliḥ) destruction, and the case of the Providence of the Real (*al-Ḥaqq*) in its warning them by the Divine tongue and finding out a way of deliverance for the believers among them, were all like the case of Noah. Both of them were warners and were inspired with a device of deliverance of the believers and were given such methods of worship as were to break the fury of Nature (*Ṭabī'ah*).

When the settlements of the people of the 'Ād were in the long and winding tracts of sand and the weather of their country was inclined to dryness and warmth, the nearest and the most suitable cause of chastisement for them was an airy punishment. Consequently, rain stopped to fall for them for a long time and, as a result of it, their cattle perished. They, then, made humble entreaties to God with the result that their angelic faculty woke up and they were taken to task for their evil actions. Had they turned like animals, they would not have been punished immediately, but because the angelic providence appeared and they (despite that) reversed its predications (*aḥkām*), and were therefore cursed. When they saw the cloud, namely, the collected matter in the sky, they took it to be a rainy cloud. In fact, it was the chastisement from God they were asking for so quickly. It was then turned into a vehement wind.

Similarly, when the settlements of the people of the Thamūd were in the mountains and their caves, the nearest chastisement for them was the earthquake and the roar. Then Ṣāliḥ prayed for their destruction. When the time of their destruction came, his self (*nafs*) assumed the aspect of destruction and the gaze of God at him also mixed up with his assumed form with his practices and tenaciously stick to his methods. They should always remember his memorable works till he becomes a constitution (*dastūr*) in bravery for them. If they will not follow him, they will certainly make a mistake in the path of bravery which (bravery) will, however, decrease in them according to their capabilities.

The followers of such a leader, again, are of many kinds. There are some among them who happen to be the foremost, highly impressed by the words of the leader and are more responsive to him than even his narrator. There are some who follow the middle course, while there are others who are unjust to themselves.

In short, the people differ in nature (*fiṭrah*) as they differ in bravery. There is one who happens to be the leader by nature. He, by necessity, is disposed to the deeds of worship, to an extent that neither any custom, nor any temper (*ṭab'*), nor any compeller can prevent him from the requirements of his natural disposition. It becomes very easy for him to do the acts of worship and follow its methods without any imitation and without any narration of a narrator. Such a person is Abraham (Ibrāhīm).

Abraham was perfect in this virtue. None before or after him was so much given over to the cultivation of this virtue as he himself was given over. The Divine sciences used to be poured on him corresponding to this virtue; and in proportion to the obedience of his heart to this virtue, it became easy for him to devote himself to *Raḥmūt* when he joined the Sublime Assembly and came under the reflection of its lights. He, on that account, was made a leader and the prophets who came after him were, thus, commanded to follow his religion.

There are persons who happen to be strong in nature (*fiṭrah*) in general, to an extent that even if they do not find a leader, they do not oppose the law of Nature, but there still remains some anxiety in their minds. When such a leader is found, they become deeply impressed by his words and understand the explanation given by him. They lose no time to hold fast and maintain his laws, elucidate what he had said in a general form and propagate his religion, as was done by all the prophets who followed the religion of Abraham, commented upon and invited people towards it.

Again, there are persons who do not find any guidance when they fail to find a leader. But, when he is found, they surely derive the fullest benefit like those who were the foremost among people in accepting the truth spontaneously.

Some persons are such that they do not come out from their error but only by an invitation urging them towards the course of Nature (*Fiṭrah*), and then they derive some kind of benefit.

Still there are persons who strongly deny the requirement of Nature and are not agreeable to it. God has set a seal on their hearts, on their ears, and has raised a barrier in front of them and from behind their backs.

When Abraham attained the vigour of his life, God gave him wisdom with the result that his natural disposition became clear to him. Thus, when he saw the star, the moon and the sun setting, he was strongly reminded by them of the fact that his Lord Who has created him is one, He educates and guides him, is free from the attributes of bodies and is above humanity. He was then overwhelmed by a strange state in which Truth became abundantly clear to him. As he was extremely jealous of things which were worshipped besides God, he broke the idols into pieces, and then, in consequence, was thrown into the fire. But he was a servant with whom God was pleased, and He desired that he should live in the world. God, then, cast a cold effect (*hai'at*) upon the matter of fire at once by means of a wind, which, coming from the frigid zone carrying extremely strong coldness, blew over it, and changed it (the fire). From this mutual clash between the burning fire and the chilly wind a fine and pleasant weather was produced.

Then he felt much distressed and disgusted with his association with people who were dissolute and were contending about the religion of God. He, therefore, migrated to his Lord, i.e. to a land where it might be possible for him to do His worship. But while he was on his way, a powerful and rebellious chief who intended to wrong him in connection with his wife opposed him and blocked his way. He then, prayed to God most earnestly,

Who, in return, inspired the angels to enter into the body of the powerful chief from where the air spreads (in the body). In consequence, his hand shrank. When he saw this, he not only left his wife free but appointed Hagar (Hājar) mother of Ishmael (Ismā'īl) as her servant.

Abraham and his wife had grown old by that time, but had not been blessed with a child. God showed mercy to him and gave him two children. It was only His pure Providence towards Abraham as he was His beloved servant. Then, a Divine attraction penetrated both of them.

The people in those days were also in need of the successors of the leader in Nature (*Fiṭrah*). The most suitable person to the leadership was one in whose natural disposition the secret of attraction (*jadhb*) had penetrated. On that account, the prophecy and the Divine Scripture were sanctioned for their offspring and inviting people towards the oneness of God (*Tauḥīd*) was prescribed as a duty for their progeny.

As regards one of his two sons (Ishmael), the intention of God was to make him the keeper of His Sanctuary (Ka'bah), and through him show His kindness to people and manifest a sign (*shi'ār*) by means of which they could seek the nearness of God, and give him offspring in which such community might come into existence as might be obedient to His commandments. The nearest cause of bringing that community into existence was that Sārah (wife of Abraham) might offer Hagar (Hājar) as a gift to Abraham who then gave birth to Ishmael. And the immediate cause of his reaching the land of the Sanctuary was the jealousy excited in Sārah. She, out of jealousy, expelled Hagar and her son from her house. Abraham, then, rehabilitated them in a barren land and God caused a spring (of water) to gush out and inspired into the hearts of some people to settle down there. This is how the administration of the Sanctuary became organised.

God inspired into the heart of Abraham to build His house (Ka'bah) and take his lodging there. He gave him insight with blessings, taught him the rites of pilgrimage and the way of His worship in the House, so that He may bless his integrity. All this settled down in his heart as a necessary revelation, which he saw reflected in the mirror of his mind.

God then managed the affair of Ishmael and appointed him as a keeper of His House and inspired the hearts of people with the desire of making pilgrimage. He also revealed to him the practice of virtues and assigned to him the duty to command his people to do good deeds.

As regards the other son, God conveyed a good news about him to Abraham by means of angels, and through them He excited the youth of Sārah, and caused her menstrual discharge to return to her, with the result that she gave birth to Isaac (Isḥāq).

It may be remembered that when Abraham devoted himself to God instinctively and naturally he was reckoned one of the angels nearest to the Throne of God. He was then addressed by the Divine man (origin of humanity) through the Sublime Assembly by the tongue of voluntariness and choice (*irādah, ikhtiyār*). It was, therefore, that he openly declared astronomy, fire-worship and polytheism as false.

God, as a matter of fact, had intended a cause by this education. And it was this that in those times the religions had differed, true investigation was lost by the fire-worshippers and in astronomy polytheism was at its top. Thus, the truth which was to break the falsehood was to follow the path of Nature and obey the tongue of voluntariness.

The events in that age used to take place as a result of the faculties of the celestial spheres and elements without any means. Enoch (Idrīs), therefore, spoke of sciences which were suitable to that age. But, thereafter, the Sublime Assembly crowded the Holy Fold (*Ḥaẓīrat al-Quds*). Each one of them (Sublime Assembly) was like a secret consisting of some faculties of the celestial spheres. When God intends to do a certain thing, He effects expansion or contraction in the Sublime Assembly and, thereby, completes His intention.[1] As no clear order (*ḥukm*) had remained with the celestial spheres at that time, Abraham came to wipe out astronomy and speak about the unity of God, and

1. Qur'ān, ii. 245 : والله يقبض ويبسط.

call people towards the Emanation (*Tajalli*) standing in the Holy Fold.

It may be known that the (Divine) sciences which are with the Sublime Assembly are the nearest ones to be poured into the minds of people bearing resemblance to the angels. Such matters as giving guidance to people, sending curse upon the disobedient among them and prescribing universal laws for them, etc., take place in the Sublime Assembly. It is, therefore, that through it the Divine sciences are revealed to the prophets in their language, and according to their perceptive faculties.

Remember that God has various tongues. When He intended to teach Abraham the way of seeking His nearness through the sacrifice of an offering, He spoke to him by two tongues so that it may remain as a great event, signifying his sincerity and obedience to God, and in order that the ransom of the son by sacrifice, according to that tongue, may continue to remain as a blessing worthy of thanks.

Now, the way towards it is that, like man, the spirits of the animals include the whole world, with this difference only that in the animal, as compared to man, it is extremely general. This secret then became clear to him and appeared to him in the dream that he should sacrifice his son who was complete and perfect. This was represented to him, just as the prescription of fifty prayers was represented to our Holy Prophet, and then afterwards only five prayers were rendered necessary. God, then, informed that His word will not change. They were five in reality and fifty in the sense that each one carried the reward of ten. Thus, they were fifty by (the tongue) of symbolism (*lisān tajawwuz*) by which God spoke in order to complete His favour and put his obedience to trial.

Similarly, God spoke to Abraham by two tongues. One of them was the tongue of symbolism, namely, that he should sacrifice his son, meaning thereby a full-grown ram, which happened to be the dearest thing to its owner as the son is dearest to his father. When he obeyed this tongue, a great event took place for him, which spoke of his worship very clearly. It was even written in his scroll that he actually sacrificed his son for the sake of God

Who, in return, ransomed him with a great sacrifice, by way of completing His favour and mercy upon them both.

The other tongue (by which He spoke to Abraham) was the tongue of reality (*lisān ḥaqīqat*). He, therefore, said: "Verily you have fulfilled the dream," [2] namely, "you made the correct interpretation of the dream and understood its meaning," and by that was meant the sacrifice of the ram and nothing else.

Abraham received from the Divine man (*Imām Nau' Insānī*) the knowledge of socio-economics and of virtue and vice. It was, therefore, that he set rules for the entertainment of the guest, the rights of the wayfarer, the natural qualities and the way of seeking the nearness of God through sacrifice. He established the principles of Islam and discarded polytheism altogether.

There was, however, Lot in his party. He had received a good training from him and had heard him well. His words had left a deep impression upon him, and this was one of his good works. But in his days, there were people who were overcome by shamelessness and immorality. They made mischief in the land, and were thus joined to the animals in the satisfaction of their bodily pleasures. As a result of it, God became angry with them, but it was, however, from the requirements of His wisdom to warn them before striking them with a punishment for their evil actions. He, therefore, revealed to Abraham to rise and warn them even through one man of his party. He, accordingly sent Lot who preached to them, reminded them of the consequences of evil deeds and gave them a warning, but it did not profit them a little. The wisdom of God then waited for the heavenly and the earthly causes to become prepared for accepting (the flow of) an airy change by which they were to be chastised. When the command of God came for execution, the angels assumed the forms of human beings and came to Abraham, as he was the real source for giving warning, and it was he in whose hands they (the angels) had placed their foreheads in the form of guests. He then offered them (food) what the guests deserve to be offered. But when he found that their hands were not reaching it, he mistrusted them and felt some fear from them, till it became clear to

2. Qur'ān, xxxvii. 105.

him that they were angels. Then the apparent fear disappeared from him and from the members of his family and, instead, cheerfulness came to them, and their minds became dyed with the dye of Divinity. On account of that it was from their prayer, "May the mercy and blessings of God be upon you, O members of the family."[3]

It may be borne in mind that the angels are from the soul (*Rūḥ*) of God, and the soul does not pass by anything, but that its life and youth return to it. They very earnestly prayed to God for blessing, namely, that the condition of Sārah be made sound. Divine mercy at that time was also waiting for accepting the prayer of Abraham. In consequence she suddenly turned up young out of joy and wonder which had overtaken her outwardly and inwardly. An effect of such good news was that when she imagined the existence of a child, her cheerfulness deeply penetrated her body. This is just like the case of a seriously sick person who is sometimes cured by a certain good news all of a sudden and just as stories of the strongly lustful strengthen the power of lust.

Then Abraham asked the angels about their intention and they informed him of it. They then went to the village of Lot, and alighted at his house as guests. There his people came to him running with the intention of mischief. God, in return, blinded them in their hurry and haste which they had made up for fighting with Lot. As the pace of their walk was quickened, the earth rolled them up.

They were then commanded not to look behind, lest they may take their journey as long. But the resolution of the people of Lot which was like a body for the Divine Soul became shattered and the chastisement followed, and that was in the form of a strong earthquake and the rain of stones of baked clay which were formed by the combination of rain, winds and cold.

It may be remembered, that all the punishments which come from the atmospheric world do not take place but only when there happen to be terrible conjunctions of the stars. They, again, do not take place but only when the rain is withdrawn in the sky and when much matter is collected both in the sky and

3. Qur'ān, li. 24-28.

the earth for a long time. Then with that atmospheric change the anger of the Sublime Assemby and its curse are joined. God then effects expansion in those causes with the result that sometimes He turns that collected matter into the form of an earthquake and a roar, at times in the shape of swallowing up by the earth and the rain of stones of baked clay, and at times in the form of a vehement wind, lightning and the spreading fire.

JOSEPH

For Joseph (Yūsuf), God had decreed trial, misfortune and separation from his father, as the heavenly causes were agreeable to that. He was, therefore, smitten by a great misfortune from the jealousy of his brothers shown towards him. For example, he was cast by them into the well and was sold by them. When he was brought to Zulaikhā (wife of Potiphar) he was thrown into prison. Finally when the period of his trial ended, God showed mercy to him and showered His blessings upon him, both open and secret. There were indeed many a favour for him from His Lord in all those happenings which happened to him. Some of those favours are as under.

(1) As Joseph was righteous and pure, he saw in his dream the favour of God which He was to bestow upon him in future, namely, that he would be obeyed by people and greatly honoured by his parents and brothers. Jacob (Ya'qūb) interpreted that dream and understood the intention of God, and, through his taking notice of the secret of His intention, also understood by regular course (*wajh muntaẓim*), that he was fit for the knowledge of the interpretation of dreams. It is so, because the dreams and the happenings have their interpretation which is known to him who is well aware of the regular course (*al-tanabbuh al-muntaẓim*); and by it is meant that the picture drawn by his imagination for the intended meaning may be of a form suitable to the nature (*ṭabī'ah*), according to the requirement of the universal nature, when it pours a general reality into the world of mortals (material world).

(2) When his brothers became jealous of him and held consultation among themselves for killing him, He moved the tongue of a man from among them to utter the words: "Do not kill Joseph but cast him down to the bottom of the well."[1] He

1. Qur'ān, xii. 10.

then made all the rest to obey his words. Thus, He changed his murder into his being cast down into the well, and made this decision easy for him to bear.

(3) When they cast him down into the well, God revealed to him what would be his and their condition, namely, that they would obey him and acknowledge his superiority and make confession of their mistake they had committed in respect of him, as they said: "Verily God has chosen you over us,"[2] in order to make his heart firm and bring joy to him in his loneliness.

(4) The natural requirement of this happening was that Joseph should lose his life, but God effected contraction in it and did not make it a cause of the real loss of life, but of a loss only in appearance, in narration, in presumption and in the form of the sorrow of Jacob.

(5) He raised a cause for the deliverance of Joseph. He, therefore, inspired into the hearts of the people of the caravan to make a diversion towards that side, and send their water-drawer to the well, under the impression that water would be available there. Thus, he (the water-drawer) came to know of Joseph, took interest in his case, looked after him with care thinking that he was an article of merchandise, while the truth was that, by it, his long life and attainment to perfection were desired.

(6) When 'Azīz purchased him, God inspired into his heart to recommend him to his wife to do good to him and also inspired into her heart to be kind and good to him. She might adopt him as a son. Here, as a matter of fact, the intention of God about him was to establish him in the land and bestow His favours on him before His other great favours.

(7) God, then, disclosed to him wisdom and knowledge without any education and showed him the upright religion clearly, even though he was surrounded by people who were unbelievers and corrupt customs were in vogue.

(8) When Zulaikhā loved him passionately and enticed him to sin while he was full-grown and physically strong, "she desired him and he would have desired her,"[3] God showed him a great proof with the result that the incentive of his chastity became excited

2. Qur'ān, xii. 91. 3. Qur'ān, xii. 24.

and it then suppressed the incentive of his temperament, even though it was strong. His father appeared to him in his imagination prohibiting him from that evil act. He (his father) was a person about whom he had the belief that he was a sign of God on earth and was the inviter to the path of truth.

(9) When Joseph was accused and there was none among men to pronounce a word of truth for him, God enabled a child to speak with wisdom, by which his immunity became clear and manifest.

(10) When the wife of 'Azīz adorned him and presented him before the women to avert the blame from herself, they fell in love with him and tried their level best to win him over. There, to preserve his chastity apparently looked impossible for him. He, therefore, prayed to his Lord to deliver him (from their mischief) even if through an imprisonment, about which Zulaikhā lost no time in threatening him in order to achieve her object. God accepted his prayer and made it look well for them to imprison him, even though the evidences were there to give the proof of his immunity.

(11) God raised a wonderful cause for his deliverance and for his establishment in the land of Egypt. He made the people, both common and the elite, to speak of him with praise and commendation, and then showed a dream to two young persons, and guided Joseph to interpret it correctly. He, then, came to know what the purpose was, and asked the cup-bearer to remember him before his master and apprise him of his merits.

(12) When the people of Egypt were smitten by a year of drought and were about to perish, God inspired into the heart of their king with a device of deliverance, as a sign of mercy towards them. That inspiration, however, was not to become complete, nor was that device to be found but through Joseph. And there was no way of deliverance for Joseph but through an inspiration and by people's standing in need of him. He, therefore, excited the need of the king and the citizens towards him and also excited his need towards them so that He might complete an affair which had to be accomplished. This is how in many happenings many Divine favours combine together for the sake of many persons.

(13) He gave support to Joseph to think of his remaining in prison, till his immunity was to become manifest, and he might have a true renown among men before the other favours of God were showered upon him, and the talk of his truthfulness spread in the world. On account of that, the Holy Prophet praised him and acknowledged his excellence when he said, "Had I stayed in the prison. . . ."[4]

(14) God made Joseph as a king and made Rayyān and the people to obey him, and made that as a favour upon him and the people.[5]

(15) He excited the desire of the brothers of Joseph to go to him, so that the meeting of the grieved might be arranged. Jacob knew the oneness of God (*tawḥīd*) and the science of all the causes as to how they are working in the universe. He, therefore, feared the attack of an evil eye and asked them to be on their guard.

(16) When Joseph desired to detain his brother with himself, in order to please himself in his company, in a way that they may not be aware, God prepared a plan for him and, thus, moved the tongue of one of his brothers to say: "He in whose bag is found the drinking-cup then he himself is the penalty for it."[6] They thought that by this statement they are clearly manifesting their immunity, while the truth was that they were unconsciously working towards the accomplishment of the object of Joseph.

Thereafter, God made a general revelation to Jacob, that he would meet his children one day. He, then, completed His favour on him, restored his eyesight to him through his cheerfulness which he felt at the hearing of this news, and, in addition, He proved the dream of Joseph to be true.

These are the signs which appeared for Joseph. It, thus, behoves the believers to learn from them as to how God manifests His favours on His creation, when He desires to save a particular person cast in danger, or to help him to attain his perfection in this world and in the Hereafter,; and when He desires to save a

4. The words of the Tradition are :
ولولبثت فى السجن مالبث يوسف لاجبت الداعى

5. Rayyān was the name of the king of Egypt.

6. Qur'ān, xii. 75.

people, how He inspires them with the device of deliverance, from destruction, and how one who is fit for that device begins to work for it. You think over the signs of God and try to understand His administration in the creation.

JOB

Job (Ayyūb) had grown up in ease, prosperity, peace, worship and cleanliness. He was sent as a prophet to his people to command them to do good and prohibit them from evil, invite them to the upright religion, and to satisfying the need of the poor and the destitute among them. Then the heavenly causes agreed to smite him with a misfortune affecting his wealth, his family and his body. In those days, he was under the favours of his Lord, Who had given him prosperity and peace of mind. This healthy change of his condition was the result of certain principles, which clearly speak of his obedience to God. This was then written in the scroll of his actions and his Lord thanked him for that.

When the period of his trial ended, his Lord showered His favours on him, and the Divine mercy which lay concealed made its full appearance. He was then asked: "Urge with thy foot; here is a cool washing-place and a drink."[1] As regards the urging, it was a favour from God shown to him through earthly causes, so that it (the urging) might not go purposeless and vain altogether. He, therefore, caused a spring to gush out and it was one of its properties to remove away leprosy, just as it is one of the properties of the spring of sulphur to remove away itching. He used it for bathing and for drinking. Then, God cured the exterior of his body and the matter of his disease also disappeared. Youth returned to him and to his wife, and they gave birth to as many children as had died before and an equal number in addition. God established for him true renown among the people of his days and even among those who came after them. He blessed his property, just as He had blessed it before many a time.

One day when he was taking a bath, locusts came to him, as a mercy from his Lord. When they alighted at his house, they

1. Qur'ān, xxxviii. 42.

turned into gold. There was only one which alighted outside the house; he coveted it knowing well that the Divine mercy when it turns towards (man) from one side it becomes necessary to seek it as far as possible.

He had made a vow that he would give one hundred strokes to his wife, while God looked at him with an eye of mercy and kindness. He, therefore, in the fulfilment of his vow became satisfied with the form of the vow against its meaning. If he had given one hundred strokes that would have meant causing a severe pain, and its alternative form was one hundred acts (*f.'lata*). This is how He deals with His beloved servants. Thus, He became contented with them by their observance of the form of the bounds of Law against their meaning as a favour from Him in connection with the universal laws which are framed by the Sublime Assembly; and also because He found that the observance of meaning would be too hard and difficult for them. Such has been His dealing in connection with every approved order (*niẓām marḍīyyah*). When voluntary causes are found agreed upon, He decides between the two (form and meaning) with justice, and remains contented with one aspect of the thing against the other.

JETHRO

Jethro (Shu'aib) was a true believer and obedient to his Lord. His people made mischief in the land and wronged people in their rights, and adopted corrupt practices. The wronged were crying for help, but no help was given to them. They had forgotten their belief in God and the Hereafter completely. Then the wisdom of God required that He should reveal to Jethro that he should warn them and apprise them of what He was going to do with them, and inform them of His curse upon them. But when his warning did not profit them at all, the Divine wisdom lay in wait; till when the rain was withheld from them for a long time and the matter of the earth also was held back and the heat grew strong, the command of God came for execution. A hot wind blew over them, and then it was further intensified with the result that it turned into fire. They were then frightened and destroyed.

Then Jethro returned as a believer, obeying his Lord as before. That agitation, however, disappeared from him which was caused in his mind by his contention with the unbelievers and his giving warning to them, the reason being that he came to know that the sending of curse upon them had already been decided in the Sublime Assembly. He used to take delight in the frequent descent of the Divine states upon his heart and, therefore, wished that, at least, some of his people could believe if some did not.

MOSES AND AARON

It may be remembered that the Pharaoh (Fir'aun) had become haughty and proud against God and His signs and had claimed himself to be a god. He had enslaved the servants of God, made mischief in the land and had oppressed the children of Isrā'īl (Banū Isrā'īl) by disregarding them and killing their sons; while they, as a matter of fact, were the best servants of God on His earth. They humbly prayed and cried to Him for help. As a result of that, God desired to punish the Pharaoh and his people for their evil deeds and show His favour to these weak ones and make them the leaders and the heirs. He, therefore, decided to create a man of a high rank through whom those tyrants were to be destroyed and these weak ones were to be saved. God had already shown many favours to Moses from the very beginning of his life up to the attainment of his young age. He had involved him in many a trial, to make manifest to him his natural disposition and clearly bring out his hidden capability (*isti'dād.*) Some of His favours on him are as follows:

(1) When the Pharaoh had sent midwives to the women of Banū Isrā'īl as spies, He kept Moses concealed from them in this way that their reasoning led them to conclude that there was no pregnant woman among them. Again, when he was born, He inspired into the heart of his mother with a device for his deliverance, saying, "Give him suck, then when thou fearest for him, cast him into the river and fear not, nor grieve; surely We shall bring him back to thee and make him one of the messengers."[1]

She had a presentinment of mind that his detention with her was an indication of the possibility of his ruination. But if he was to be cast down into the river it might be the cause of his deliverance, and perhaps he might be that same person about whom

1. Qur'ān, xxviii. 7.

the learned of Banū Isrā'īl had given good news, and the one from whom the Pharaoh feared.

Then the inspiration into her heart appeared in the form of a thought. That thought again was blessed with the result that it prevailed upon her to an extent that she could not control herself and did that work, namely, threw the box which contained her child into the river. God caused the waves to rise in fury in the river till it (river) threw off the box by (the palace of) the family of the Pharoah, which was then picked up by them. He inspired them with the desire to take interest in him, and they were thus thinking that he might benefit them or they might adopt him as a son.

Here the plain truth was that God desired to give a good training to Moses and keep him safe from the fear of the Pharaoh. Such has been His course whenever He desired to raise a community or a nation. Sometimes, He tempts an immoral man to do a certain thing suitable to his intellect. This is how God accomplishes His object while that man does not know. On that account, the Holy Prophet has said, "Verily God strengthens this religion by an immoral man."[2]

"The heart of the mother of Moses then became free (from fear),"[3] but as she was not stripped off from the predication of nature (*ṭabī'ah*), she could not obey the inspiration properly. Her thinking prevailed upon her, and she realised that she had made a mistake in planning, It was necessary for her to have searched out the box before the waves could deliver him. God strengthened her heart, and she, therefore, at times used to say that perhaps God might do what she was hoping for, and at times was wishing to disclose her secret out of anxiety.

She said to his sister: " 'Follow him up.' So she watched him from a distance while they perceived not."[4] Then God desired that "her eyes be made cool and she should not grieve."[5] And that she should give suck to Moses without any fear of the Pharaoh, so that he might be served more kindly and with much reliance because of his relationship. Besides, it would be more near to the upright

2. *Ṣaḥīḥ Bukhārī* (aṣ-Ṣaḥ-ul-Maṭābi', Karachi), Vol. II, p. 604.

3. Qur'ān, xxviii. 10. 4. Qur'ān, xxviii. 11. 5. Qur'ān, xx. 40.

religion he had adopted. And at the same time it would be a Divine favour to her, in order that she might know that the thought which was created in her heart was an inspiration from her Lord, so that she may obey and thank Him, as that would be more profitable for her in her perfection.

God raised a cause and deprived Moses of his sucking of the breasts of the midwives with the result that he was not sucking any breast but was finding its milk as tasteless, until this behaviour of his tired them (Pharaoh and his family). They were then guided to her (the mother of the child) and he too found her milk palatable and sweet, and then she was appointed as his nurse.

(2) Moses continued progressing in his knowledge and in his intellect, and his natural disposition also became clear to him. Till when he attained his young age, God gave him wisdom and knowledge. He, then, understood the interpretation of the universal laws and became fit to be dyed with the dye of the Sublime Assembly. Then God desired to free Moses from the supervision of the Pharaoh and deliver him from him, so that he should be more perfect in his knowledge and direction. As Moses was of those the expansion of whose natural disposition could become complete through the company of the believers, and in order to prevent him to a certain extent from the socio-economic system of the haughty and the proud and their company, God desired to keep him away from the Pharaoh.

God then raised a cause which did not clash with his immunity from sin. It happened in this way that he once intervened between two persons who were fighting between themselves, with the intention of bringing peace between them. There he was, however, dragged to punish the unjust, so he hastened to kill him. But afterwards he prayed to his Lord for forgiveness in the language he knew that day. God forgave him and removed away that disorderly state of his mind, namely, that he had committed an offence; while he, as a matter of fact, in his killing the unjust, was serving the command of God and obeying Him. But the language of his times and his own condition required that he should not understand this secret, and the commandments of the *Sharī'ah* which he had understood should also remain confused to him. He, therefore, became fearful.

(3) Then God moved the tongue of one whom Moses had helped and shown favour to utter words which implied the fear of the loss of his life. It was, in fact, a device from God, so that it might become a cause for his exit and for his despair from the ease and comfort which he enjoyed at the hands of the Pharaoh. It happened like this. The Pharaoh had understood from the words of Moses, "Verily you are clearly in error,"[6] that "He desires to seize him."[7] He became angry, and gave out this news which spread throughout the city. God then made the reporter of the news to say what urged him (Moses) to leave the country.

(4) When he set out for Midian without provision, without a beast for riding and without any guide, and entrusted his affairs to God and placed his reliance upon Him, He also, in turn, took the responsibility of his protection and guidance. When he reached the watering-place of Midian God raised a cause, in order to establish him in that land (of Midian). He inspired into the heart of Moses to give water to the sheep of Jethro (Shu'aib) voluntarily and also inspired into the heart of Jethro and his two daughters with the desire to take interest in him, as he was constitutionally strong and trustworthy. This is how God accomplished His object with regard to both of them as He liked.

(5) He then guided Moses to select a rod from a lot, which had been inherited by the prophets one after another and which was a blessed one. Then Moses left the city making for Egypt, apparently out of love for his people, while, as a matter of fact, God had to execute the order of the conveyance of the Message (*Risālah*).

(6) When he reached the valley of Ṭuwā which was a blessed valley where the spiritualities of the angels had gathered, God raised a cause with the result that he stood in the need of fire and some news. His wife was overtaken by the pangs of childbirth, coldness came in at the same time, and he lost the way. When he reached a lote tree in that valley, God made a wonderful manifestation to him, the like of which had never been narrated to have been made to anyone before. It happened like this.

6. Qur'ān, xxxiii. 18.

7. Qur'ān, xxviii. 19.

The Sublime Assembly desired to speak to Moses face to face. He was a man of hard nature (*ṭabī'ah*) and extraordinarily brave. When he thought of fire very strongly, God manifested the form of fire, not made of the elements (*ṭabā'i'*), but was sent purely from the Similitudinary World. Then, He spoke to him verbally in that fire itself, through the language of the Sublime Assembly. Hearing that speech, Moses feared, but God cheered Him and ordered him to go to the Pharaoh and invite him towards faith. He also showed him the miracle of the rod and the white hand.

The truth about the rod and the (white) hand is that the Similitudinary World, as it appears in respect of its existence, is independent, and is not connected with any material existence like fire. Similarly, when it sparingly appears in a material body, it (the material body) acquires its attribute. The similitudinary existence then prevails upon it with the result that the material rod turns into the non-material (similitudinary) one, and its two ends become like the two hoods of a snake. Similar is the case of the hand. There was a flutter of light in it, which afterwards became light itself.

The magic in those times used to influence the minds of people to such an extent that they began to think of such attributes and states in the material objects which they actually did not possess. The truth, therefore, appeared in that similar form (namely, magic). The magic, in fact, is a falsehood, because it is simply an imagination without any foundation, while this (which comes from the Similitudinary World) is a truth which has a foundation. God, on that day, made manifest to him (Moses) all the favours which were done to him, for example, when He made revelation to his mother and when He poured His love on him, etc., right up to his present state. He taught him the principles of worship and the way to dispute with the Pharaoh.

(7) Moses had asked for certain things, like the removal of the impediment of his tongue and that his brother be made his minister. God granted all he had asked for. When Moses began to argue with the Pharaoh, there followed many favours of God for him, because he was His beloved servant with whom He was pleased. And there also followed the signs such as the curse of

God on the Pharaoh and on his people.

(8) When the Pharaoh asked him about his Lord, he answered him by the clearest of His signs, because the knowledge of the Essence (*Dhāt*) of God is known but to very few persons only. The Divine Laws are, however, universal, applicable to all the people. The Pharaoh then demanded from Moses a sign with the result that the rod turned out to be a snake, and when he drew out his hand it looked white. He, thus, baffled the magicians and the truth appeared clear and bright.

(9) When the Pharaoh decided to kill Moses, God made a believer from his family to admonish them (family of the Pharaoh) and remind them of the consequences of the disobedience of the prophets, till he restrained them from their decision and put them into doubt about their affair. He then inspired into their hearts the idea of postponing the matter of Moses and sending for the magicians for his opposition, thinking that their word would be raised thereby, while, as a matter of fact, it was a cause for raising the word of Moses and for the appearance of his miracle.

(10) God guided the magicians towards the path of truth, so that it might render his (Moses's) argument even more explicit, as those who had tried to oppose him became obedient to him.

(11) God had tried them through nine clear signs.[8] Whenever Moses prayed to God for their removal, He removed them and whenever he prayed to Him to send them down upon them, they were duly sent down by Him.

(12) When He commanded Moses to go out with his followers to the river, the Pharaoh and his army followed them. And when they reached the river, God caused a violent wind to blow upon it (river), which divided one part of it from the other and rendered that divided part as dry, and acted freely in its other part as it (wind) acts freely in the parts of the earth when it turns into the form of a storm. This is how He saved Banū Isrā'īl and destroyed the Pharaoh and his army.

Again, when they set out towards Jerusalem, they happened to pass by a people who were given to the worship of idols. There the foolish among his followers in whose heart the sweetness of

8. Qur'ān, xvii. 101.

faith had not entered as yet asked him (Moses): "Fix for us a god as they have gods (fixed) for them,"[9] the reason being that their disposition was wanting in paying attention towards Divinity. When Moses delivered strong sermons to them, they asked for a form of Divinity through which to pay their attention to it. Moses, then, acquainted them with the truth and put them to shame. They were then restrained forcibly, but remained silent in doubt about their affair. Sāmirī understood that from them and he did with them what he did.[10]

(13) God promised Moses to speak to him secretly in a blessed spot of land, give him the tablets and the commandments. The selection of a particular spot of land was made, because the spiritualities of the angels had gathered there. Moses confined himself to that place, exclusively devoted himself to the remembrance of God and, thus, acquired resemblance to Divinity.

When he saw the place where God made a manifestation, he submitted to that state and was moved by it. God gave him the tablets on which guidance and mercy were written, in other words, sermons, the attributes and the clear works of God, and also an account of the days of prosperity and adversity which God brings to people by turns. The essence of the tablets was of the green emerald of Paradise, namely, of the essence resembling the emerald which God had created by His word "*Kun*" (Be) without any material cause.

Sāmirī misguided Banū Isrā'īl after the departure of Moses for the Ṭūr mountain by casting a handful of the footprints of the Spirit (*ar-Rūḥ*, Gabriel) into the image of a calf, the property of which was that when it passed into a thing, a suitable life returned to it. That, as a matter of fact, was a mercy and an honour shown towards the virtuous men of Banū Isrā'īl which they actually deserved, against their foolish ones.

It is so because there were persons among them who were liars by nature, had turned to the worship of others than God, and the thoughts of their unbelief were dominating them time

9. Qur'ān, vii. 138.

10. Sāmirī was the contemporary of Moses, and was a magician who had made a speaking calf.

after time. God, therefore, desired to purify Banū Isrā'īl from them. There were also persons among them who, if they had lived in the world, would never have turned towards the reality of faith, as their earthly nature had prevented them from that. Their good, therefore, lied in this that they should be killed in their state of obedience to God so that their souls make a progress in the Intermediary World. Moses, then, summoned Sāmirī, removed the doubt and cursed him.

(14) Some people defamed Moses saying that he suffered from rupture, because he used to cover himself during his taking the bath out of shame. They took this act of his as an attempt on his part to hide his defect. God, then, cleared him from what they had said about him. He was indeed worthy of respect with God, and He did not like that he should be defamed. Thus, when once he passed by a watering-place and desired to take a bath, he placed his clothes on a stone, and that stone rolled them down the earth till he was seen (when he ran to catch them) by the people of Banū Isrā'īl as naked, and there they testified his freedom from rupture.

(15) When Moses saw that the Divine Providence had turned towards him fully and completely, and he also had acquired strong resemblance to the Sublime Assembly, he prayed to God to show Himself to him openly, i.e. he might see His light when the Universal Soul penetrated into the fifth element (namely, of the Similitudinary World) and assumed therein a form of a luminous body imitating the extent of his knowledge about his Lord, so that its (luminous body's) soul might become an introduction and acquaint him of the Real (God). Itself, and its body might be made of the world of the Sublime Assembly, and there the blend of both the soul and the body become of such nature that the relation of the state of one could be correctly applied to that of the other, as is the case of the otherworldly body which would combine both the material and the immaterial aspects. This is the meaning of the Word of God: "Show me (Thyself), so that I may have a look at Thee."[11]

11. Qur'ān, vii. 143.

This act, however, did not proceed from Moses but only when he came to know of the freedom of action of the Primal Soul when it happens to take care of the guidance of one of the beloveds, as it happened for him during his love of the fire. Moses, from the very beginning of his life, was Divinely supported in his paying attention towards the Real (*al-Ḥaqq*), but he was not supported with the freedom to act through the Real in the creation (*khalq*). It is, therefore, that the Real on that day, because of his fiery temperament, appeared to him in the form of a fire, but it did not burn him. And if He were to appear today, He will appear in the shape of a burning fire, which, when it will touch a thing, will destroy it through, the reason being that it was the form of Moses himself reflected in the mirror of the Real. Moses, then, understood that God does not manifest Himself to anything but in the form of that thing itself reflected in the mirror of the Real. That thing, then, according to its capability, becomes a necessary cause for the appearance of the form of the Real. Here you make an exception in the case of the prophets as they cannot be ignorant of such kind of knowledge, because their knowledge is perfect. Moses never knew that he on that day was in such a state that if God had manifested Himself in His very form his body would have been completely destroyed. However, by his survival it was the intention of God to show mercy to people. God, therefore, showed mercy to him and appeared to him on a mountain, but the mountain broke to pieces and Moses fell in a swoon. When he recovered, that subtle point became clear to him and he, therefore, repented to God saying that, in future, he would ask by his tongue according to his capability.

(16) The people of Moses also demanded what he himself had demanded (namely, to see God openly). The reflection of his longing (state) towards the phenomena of the Universal Soul fell upon their minds as well with the result that the Real appeared in the form of a thunderbolt which destroyed them. Then God brought them to life again, a sign of His mercy towards Moses, and then commanded them to settle in the holy land (Jerusalem) which He gave to them as gift.

The holy land, however, was under the control of a people

who were tyrannical and powerful. They (the people of Moses) were, therefore, commanded to wage war against them and were given the promise of victory. Moses, then, took from every tribe its headman to inquire about them (tribe people), command them to do good, prohibit them from evil and make a distinction between people according to their character. He (Moses) then sent some of them as spies to the tyrants. Two of them gave news (about the strength of the enemy) which encouraged them to fight, while all the rest gave information which was making them cowardly. He forgave these two, and Moses took them as his trustworthy caliphs. God became angry with the others and destroyed them.

(17) Now when the reports differed, Banū Isrā'īl lost their hearts from fighting with them. God, then, blamed them and, for some time, made them to lose the path in the desert, where they could not find the way out. The consumption of their provisions put them into difficulty. Moses, therefore, prayed to God with his utmost devotion with the result that He provided them with manna and quails as a subsistence, which He had produced by effecting contraction and expansion in the causes. He made for them a thick cloud resembling darkness to protect them against sunshine, and also a bright fire looking like columns to suffice them against the firebrands and lamps. He blessed their clothes, which, in turn, were neither becoming ugly, nor were getting worn out. All this was the result of God's acting freely in the matter of clouds and lightning. Such changes have examples in the nature (*ṭabī'h*) as well.

(18) Moses received an inspiration in the light of which whenever he struck a rock which was the fittest one in being capable of giving water, it was getting split up, and water used to come out from it. He was then dividing it (water) into twelve springs according to the number of the tribes.

(19) There was, however, a man among the tyrannical and the powerful who had known the sciences (*'ulūm*) of the prophets and had remembered their books by heart. Unfortunately, he became obedient to the devil and inclined towards worldly life. He asked them to send harlots to Banū Isrā'īl to mingle up with

them, so that impiety among them might increase, the blessing might disappear and the flow of Divine Providence might stop. The reason of it was this that, though the Divine Providence, because of the dearness of Moses and Hārūn to God, required that aid should be given to them, the prevalence of evil upon them (Banū Isrā'īl) required that they should be deserted. Moses was, therefore, supported by God to drive out the harlots.

They (Moses and his followers), then, fought with the tyrants and God gave them victory in their conquering that country, where He rehabilitated them. They lived there undisturbed, except when they did any wrong they were punished for that. He made them kings on the earth living a luxurious life and united them through Moses. He (Moses) was teaching them the Pantateuch, preaching them, purifying them, setting up religious limits for them and was exacting justice for the wronged from the wrong-doer. Such has been the dealing of God with His dear servants. He makes the worldly life easy for them to live and establishes for them true renown and acceptance among people. If the people agree to place their reliance upon Him, and obey Him without hesitation and without divided minds, God would surely give them subsistence from Himself, and bless their standing corn, their cattle and their earnings.

(20) God, besides other things, taught Moses the art of alchemy. This news by chance reached Qārūn who was his cousin. He became wealthy through learning that art, but, in turn, transgressed, grew oppressive and forgot both the beginning and the end. He was no doubt a tyrant. Moses prohibited him from the working of mischief, but he was not checked, and on the contrary harboured rancour against him, and accused him of prostitution. He, therefore, cursed him very strongly, with the result that God made the earth to swallow him and his house.

This was one of the signs of God, so that the people may know how He deals with him who rises in pride against His prophets, harbours rancour against them, is pleased with the worldly life and forgets the rights of God. On such occasions, God chooses that form of punishment which happens to be the nearest to the natural causes on that day. His house being swallowed up on that day was the nearest form of punishment.

Moses, however, was under the impression that he was the most learned of people and, therefore, gave up further acquisition of knowledge. God intended to bring about an event which might encourage him to seek more knowledge; as He, for example, in the case of our Holy Prophet sufficed with this command, saying: "Say: O my Lord, increase me in knowledge."[12]

It happens in this way that, when the Real (*al-Ḥaqq*) manifests Itself in the form of that time (according to the requirement of the occasion), and those sciences which that manifestation requires are represented before the servant in suitable forms and shapes, he often-times does not know any other science except those ones. He neither rejects them (other sciences) nor affirms them, but simply forgets them all. In this way he goes on progressing stage by stage to a degree God likes for him. The dear one generally does not experience any extraordinary restlessness or longing.

(21) One day Moses stood up to deliver a lecture, teaching people what God had taught him, till he greatly moved the hearts of the audience. There a questioner asked him, "O Moses, do you find anyone else more learned than thee?" He replied in the negative. God then revealed to him saying: "Yes, there is Our servant Khiḍr, who knows more than thee," meaning thereby, in the knowledge of the Divine Administration (*al-Tadbīr al-Ilāhī*) as to how it works at particular times, and how he (that servant) becomes an instrument for Him to be used when He desires to complete a part of the Administration. Moses, however, was more learned than him in the knowledge of the Universal Laws and the laws which are prescribed for the people in general, and in his being the instrument of God used for the establishment of religion. Moses, therefore, asked for a way leading towards him. He was inspired that the way leading towards him would be shown to him by a salted fish. He, however, could not understand the reason of its showing the way towards Khiḍr.

Moses and a young man Joshua (Yūsha') set out in search of him. They carried with themselves some cakes of barley, a salted

12. Qur'ān, xx. 114.

fish in a basket and travelled on till they reached a rock. Moses, on account of fatigue, went to sleep while Joshua sat down to perform ablution. Some drops of water somehow fell on the fish and it came to life again. It then hurriedly ran into the sea and a dry line of its passage visibly appeared. It is so because the water has the property of bringing life to the aquatic animals. That property was blessed (made more effective) by God. Then by means of that sign they succeeded in finding Khiḍr.

(22) Then what happened to Moses and Aaron (Hārūn) is that Khiḍr showed to Moses three events which were to take place. God had raised a cause for them to effect improvement in His creation, and made one of His servants an instrument of truth for the accomplishment of the desired object. The Divine Laws (*Nawāmis*, pertaining to *Sharā'i'*) depend upon the Universal Laws and the occasions indicative of wisdom, while the causes (*Taqrībāt*) are based on the particular expediencies and the decree (*Qaḍā'*) comes into effect at every suitable time. These are, however, the most abstruse sciences and none knows them but he who becomes an instrument of the Real, and then understands the actual secret underlying that event.

Moses forgot this science many a time: firstly, when he asked for the sight of God; secondly, when he asked for forgiveness for the murder of a Copt; and, thirdly, when he argued with Adam, even though he was the most learned of people in the knowledge of the Divine Laws. It was, therefore, the wisdom of God to show him what had happened to him. Khiḍr removed a plank of the boat from fear lest the cruel king may seize it by force. God, however, protected the boat from sinking in this way, that whenever a wave passed by it, it (boat) gathered force in its flow with the result that the surface of water was not torn off. He (Khiḍr) murdered a man who had not murdered any person, because that man was born as an unbeliever. And even if he had lived, the predications of his disposition would have dominated him and he would have oppressed his parents by transgression and ingratitude. God, therefore, supported them (parents) with good. Khiḍr then raised the wall in order to protect the property which was deposited by the dear, virtuous servant.

(23) One of the great events which took place in the days of Moses was that God desired to show mercy to that young man who had shown filial pity to his mother. His father had entrusted him to God, and He in turn became responsible for his affair from his very childhood. When he became young He desired to complete His favour on him. He wished to punish that one who had murdered his relative, by depriving him of the right of inheritance, by putting him to ignominy and by killing him in return. He also desired to show mercy to Banū Isrā'īl so that they might know that the command of God and His promise of raising the dead to life are true; and they should know that when Moses had ordered them for the doing of a certain thing which, though it was apparently found difficult to accomplish, was but necessary for them to have obeyed his order, as there was a secret behind it, which was to be disclosed afterwards. And in addition, they might know that the practising of rigidity and going too deep in the (observance of the) commandments of God is a bad behaviour. Then God, through that favour, brought that known event to completion.

(24) When Moses died, He looked after Banū Isrā'īl and managed their affairs very well. He sent prophets to them so that they might warn them, give them good news, preach them, command them to do good and prohibit them from evil. All that was done according to the power given to them.

There flourished one among them who became a king, like Joshua (Yūsha'). Others became doctors in religion as Isaiah (Asha'yā), Elisha (Yasa') and Samuel (Shamwail). Besides, some others became monks strong in spiritual exercises like Elias (Ilyās). All this (the advent of such persons) was according to the requirement of expediency (*maṣliḥah*) and the selection of the nearest and the easiest cause at every time.

The prophets are descended from one and the same father, but from various mothers. Their father is one, and by that is meant the Divine Education suitable to prophecy; and their mothers are various, and by that is meant the God-given and acquired capabilities.

Whenever the people obeyed the Pentateuch and kept to it,

God blessed them; but when they disobeyed it, He punished them. And whenever they were surrounded by a calamity, He inspired them with the means of deliverance. This is the Divine course which will continue as such, if there is no obstruction.

SAMUEL, DAVID, SOLOMON AND JONAH

God had informed in the Pentateuch that the Banū Isrā'īl would soon gain prevalence, would twice make mischief and disbelieve. Every time very powerful servants (given to terrible warfare) were sent against them who entered the very inmost parts of (their) houses. When the first of the warnings came to pass, they disobeyed the injunctions of the Pentateuch. God, in consequence, appointed Goliath (Jālūt) over them. He murdered some of them and captured the others and deprived them of that box which contained sacred relics of the family of Moses and Aaron (Hārūn). They became grieved, repented and returned to their Prophet Samuel (Shamwail) and requested him for the appointment of a king for them. They knew very well that the fight with the enemy who happened to be superior in number was not possible but through the unanimity of the opinion of all, and the leadership of a person always engaged in looking after the good of the country.

It, however, becomes necessary in the wisdom of God to repel the unbelievers in a way He may like; but for repelling them He prefers to inspire the believers to fight with them. He will, no doubt, strengthen them in that fight, encourage them to bravery and will make them prevail upon the enemy. This He did by raising the cause which was nearest at that time to the natural expediencies. There were many a favour of God in that event. Some of those favours are as follows:

(1) When Saul (Ṭālūt) became king they found fault with him saying that he had no precedence, neither in kingdom nor in wealth. The Prophet Samuel (Shamwail) dispelled their doubt by telling them that it was necessary to obey the inspiration of God in relation to the Administration He carries on in the creation, but it did not benefit them. God, then, showed them a sign with which they were, however, satisfied. That sign was that the box containing the sacred relics of Moses and Aaron would come

to them, being carried by the angels. That happened in this way. They (the enemies of Banū Isrā'īl) were tried through misfortunes of famine and mutual quarrels among them. The angels then inspired them that they had been put to trial because of the box. They, then, carried it keeping it away from themselves, going from village to village, till when they brought it near the houses of Banū Isrā'īl, they placed it on a cart (pulled by bullocks) and diverted it towards them for the purpose of harming them.

As a matter of fact, therein was a cause for them. When the box came to them of its own accord, it became a sign (of blessing) for them. They felt happy at the sacred relics of Moses and Aaron and in the wake of that happiness there came calmness, tranquillity and the acknowledgment of the fact that the king (Saul) was supported and blessed by the Unseen (God).

(2) When Saul (Ṭālūt) stood in need of knowing the condition of his army, their ranks in bravery, and the strength of their hearts, so that he might rely upon everyone according to his ability, he could not find a way to that knowledge, as he was in an extreme hurry; while such kind of knowledge is gained by experience and through long association. God, therefore, showed them a river and tried them by it. He prohibited them from drinking its water save a mere sip out of their hands. This was apparently a cause for making sure of them, knowing the strength of their hearts, their penetration into the dangers and ascertaining as to how far their nature (*ṭabī'ah*) obeyed the commandments of the Divine Wisdom. However, in the judgment of reason, it (this way of trial) is not necessarily an act of bravery or a part of obedience to the king.

God, however, blessed that event with the result that the incentive of obedience did not spring up but only in the minds of those who were perfect in bravery and obedience. Thus, Saul (Ṭālūt) came to know of the brave and the obedient among them. When they went out for fight with Goliath (Jālūt) who had come with a numerous army and great pomp, he did not trust any save those in whom he had found those requisite qualities.

(3) God desired that David (Dāwūd) should have true renown among the children of Isrā'īl (Banū Isr'āil), and that he should be the ruler of the country. He, therefore, caused a stone to speak

out, namely, He disclosed its condition. Thus, when he walked over it, he heard from it that it was an instrument, meant for killing Goliath. At the same time, He also created unrest in the mind of Saul to an extent that he made it a condition that whosoever will kill Goliath will be given half of the country and his daughter in marriage. God then strengthened the heart of David and put his hand carrying stones opposite to the nostrils of Goliath, and then commanded the wind to carry those stones straight to them (the nostrils). This is how He destroyed Goliath through that plan and fulfilled His intention of help to Banū Isrā'īl, such as the repelling of the unbelievers, raising the name of David and making him the king.

David was an extremely brave man. He possessed the strong qualities of the rulership of the country. God made him a caliph in the earth and gave him leadership (*Imāmah*), committed Banū Isrā'īl to his care and declared his right on them. In addition to that, it was written in the Sublime Assembly that if they disobeyed him, they disobeyed God, and if they obeyed him, they obeyed God. He managed their affairs well, set up the limits of religion, fought with the unbelievers, settled the difficult problems, showed the signs of God and brought unity among the various tribes of Banū Isrā'īl.

David had a wonderful way of worship and humbleness to God. God inspired him with Psalms (Zabūr). Its contents were one hundred and fifty hymns. Every hymn was an invocation, an imploration and a prayer for the good of this world and of the Hereafter, and the seeking of protection with God. He was fortunately dexterous. God, therefore, inspired him with the art of making coats-of-mail, as a mercy from Him, so that it might be a source of ample subsistence for him, and a mercy to the people as well, in order that they (coats-of-mail) might protect them at the time of their fight with the enemy.

God had made reading easy for him. Thus, he was reading as much in a time as others could not read it, the reason being that He had blessed his tongue as well as his thinking power. He was thinking of every word in a clear way in a moment and was uttering words quickly according to that thinking. He made his voice sweet which used to affect both the men and the animals. He also made the mountains to obey him. It was, therefore, that when he used to sing the glory of God, they responded to him both in the morning and in the evening. It happened in this way that they used to resound like the resounding of the dome when a cry is made in it. That resounding was then blessed with the result that the words were coming out of it (resounding) of their own accord.

The real cause behind it is that when a sublime person with strong concentration is filled with a certain state, the effect of that state of his mind passes on to the other persons and to the objects of Nature around him as well. Thus, when he hears some word of wisdom from a stone or a tree required by that occasion, the power of his concentration penetrates the minds of people, and then they begin to hear what he himself had heard.

David possessed a melodious voice and a charming nature. That nature was then blessed. By his every breath a natural impression was caused. Again, his breaths were blessed; thus, a sweet rhyme was produced and it was the hymn of David.

Many a wonderful happening happened to David. Some of them are as under:

(1) Once, when his eyes fell upon a beautiful woman by chance, he loved her very strongly. He was a man who by his strong constitution (*mizāj*) was extremely passionate and lover of women. He, however, did not behave well in his cherishing a desire for marriage with her and did not take notice of the limit fixed for him in the Divine Law. God drew his attention towards that in this way that the angels appeared before him in the form of litigants. One of them said: "This is my brother. He has ninety-nine ewes while I have a single ewe. Then he said: 'Make it over to me,' and he has prevailed against me in dispute." [1] Then, exactly the same form which his mind (*nafs*) had acquired appeared in the Similitudinary World, and, with it, the anger of God also appeared against him. David understood that the interpretation of this dream was to draw his attention to what he had done. He, therefore, prayed to His Lord for forgiveness, returned

1. Qur'ān, xxxviii. 23.

to Him and held fast to the acts of redemption, till God forgave him.

(2) One night, when he was busy in the remembrance of his Lord, he found the angels descending upon Jerusalem, while, as a matter of fact, it had been demolished long ago during the days of Goliath, and no trace of it had remained. There was kept a great secret in Jerusalem as it was kept in the Ka'bah. God pointed out to him the site of the House as He had pointed out to Abraham (the place of the Ka'bah). As he had fought for the sake of God most properly, it was written in his scroll that he would demolish many structures of God. He was, thus, not able to complete the House of God but by way of service, and not by way of taking revenge and showing anger. He, therefore, prayed to God that he might complete it, as a part of (his) good action.

(3) In the days of David people exceeded the limits of Law (*Sharī'ah*), while, in the Divine Law revealed to Moses, it was prescribed for them to observe the sanctity of Saturday (Sabbath) carefully, but, in spite of that, they hunted the fish on that day with the result that God transformed them into the form of apes. That transformation took place in this way that God made the fish of corruptive constitution (*mizāj*) and of putrifactive nature (*ṭabī'ah*). Thus, when they ate it, the corruption of its constitution passed on to them. Their bodies also changed and the production of *Nasmah* (animal spirit) in them also changed. This change slowly and gradually reached its extreme limit and the hair grew on their bodies. In addition, God covered them with abasement and humiliation with the result that they turned apes. This kind of punishment (being the nearest to the then natural causes) was the most suitable for them at that time, and they were subsequently punished for their wrongdoing. It was indeed a warning for the inhabitants of that town and for those who succeeded them.

(4) He humbly prayed to God for the grant of a child who might succeed him. He accepted his prayer and granted him Solomon (Sulaimān), who was sagacious, religious, wise and good-mannered. He became his partner in settling the difficult problems

and could understand the relative good behind the particular cases.

The sheep of one party pastured in the cultivation of the other party at night. They came to David and referred their case to him. He decided it according to what had come in the Divine Law about the causing of loss, but in that there was much harm for the owner of the sheep in particular. God had explained to Solomon what the relative good was in that particular case. Many of the decisions of Solomon were of this nature.

Solomon was also given the knowledge of the socio-economic system (*irtifāq*) of the second and the third grade. David appointed him as his successor for his people, and he was also given the knowledge of understanding the speech of birds.

The truth about it is that the birds and the animals possess usual knowledge with which they are inspired whenever they stand in need of something. Sometimes, God desires a certain thing in which lies the good of the animals, such as freedom from some difficulty and the obtainment of some good. Consequently, their hearts at that time are inspired accordingly

Sometimes, when God desires to teach something to a servant, He appoints a bird and inspires it, and, thus, teaches him by means of the bird, as had happened in the story of the Hoopoe.

Birds have many voices pointing to the conditions happening to them, such as anger, fear and hunger. God had taught Solomon many of these sciences, relating to the voice of the birds.

At times, God teaches a certain gnostic something from that (knowledge of the speech of birds, etc). These things also have their particular causes which can hardly be mentioned precisely.

God also made both the wind and the Jinnis to obey him, and that happened in this way. There exists a power in air and in fire for subsisting water, which is the first element. Thus, by a certain subsisting power a thing becomes air and by some other one it becomes water and so on.

The perfect servant, at times, happens to bear resemblance to one of those powers. Solomon bore resemblance to the power of air and fire and, in addition, his mind was strongly concentrative, compelling the thing to obey him. That concentration, on account of that resemblance, was blessed (made more strong and effective). Thus, he compelled the Jinni who were building for him the synagogues and the images he liked and were diving in the sea and doing some other work besides. When he sat on the throne and ordered the wind, it carried him to where he liked.

Many wonderful happenings happened to Solomon. Some of them are as follows:

(1) One day, when the horses were presented before him they struck him with wonder so much so that he missed the time of his prayer. This made him terribly angry and he, therefore, killed and hamstrung all of them.

(2) He felt very much distressed on account of the neglect on the part of chiefs towards his orders for fight. He, therefore, wished to have intercourse with his wives, so that each one of them may give birth to a hero, waging war in the path of God. He, thereby, stuck to the worldly means and forgot to entrust this affair to God and seek His help. The gnostic, however, does not stick to the means till he pleads to God for help before that, and sees the Divine Administration working through them. God drew his attention to this fact that they (his wives) will not give birth at all. He rendered his semen thin through his frequent intercourse with the result that no complete form of child was ever made but only a part of it, cast off (by the mother). Then, that incomplete body was placed on his throne. There he came to know of the secret. He, therefore, repented to God, begged Him for support in the kingdom and said, "O my Lord, forgive me and grant me a kingdom which is not fit for anyone after me." [2]

(3) Once when he was in an extreme hurry he passed by a valley of ants. There, one ant said, "O ants, enter your houses lest Solomon and his army may crush you."[3] She said this by way of precaution according to the extent of her knowledge; Solomon, however, heard her, understood her speech and thanked God for his being given the knowledge to understand the speech of animals.

(4) When he searched the birds he did not find Hoopoe among

2. Qur'ān, xxxviii. 35. 3. Qur'ān, xxvii. 18.

them. He, therefore, held out a threat to it; but God gave it (Hoopoe) a wonderful knowledge, by way of mercy towards it, so that it might get rid of the threat. It was also a mercy towards Solomon, in order that it may be easy for him to conquer the country of Bilqīs.[4] Besides, it was a mercy towards Bilqīs and her people as well, so that they may believe. The Divine Wisdom on that day, however, required that God might inform Solomon of the real condition of Bilqīs through the tongue of Hoopoe. It (Hoopoe) pointed out to him that she was an unbeliever, possessed enormous wealth and was very beautiful. All this was done with a view to reminding Solomon of those Divine favours where were concealed in that matter.

(5) God stripped the throne of Bilqīs from the material predications and gave it the predication of the Similitudinary World instead. Thereafter, due to the prayer of one pious servant of Solomon, He put on it (throne} the material dress in that place. Solomon contrived a device to know by it the intellect of Bilqīs and her beauty, because he desired to marry her. The throne was then thrown upside down, but Bilqīs understood and Solomon succeeded in seeing her leg and found her as the most beautiful woman.

The kingdom continued to remain in the hands of the family of David. Whenever any king of some country attempted at prevailing upon them, God revealed to their prophets assuring them of His promise of victory. He, therefore, used to raise a wonderful cause for their victory. Sometimes He caused the most violent wind to blow against their faces with the result that their arrows did not hit Banū Isrā'īl. At times, when they started to fight, He smote them with terrible heat and hunger, as a consequence of which they turned cowardly and perished. On certain occasions, He excited enmity among them, and they then fought among themselves and this fighting continued for years together.

(6) The inhabitants of Nineveh (Nīnawā) revolted and rebelled. The wisdom of God required that He might command Isaiah (Asha'yā), the prophet of that age, to give them the warning even if through a man of his party. He, therefore, sent Jonah (Yūnus)

4. Name of the Queen of Sheba.

and chose him in particular because his existence was the result of the generosity and favour of God, as he was born after his parents had grown old, by way of an extraordinary course. Besides, the Divine Providence always accompanied him. God became responsible for his affairs from his very childhood. He inspired animals and wild beasts to give him suck; and also became responsible for the affair of his marriage. That marriage was brought about in this way, that God showed this one in the dream what prompted him to ask that man's daughter in marriage and showed that one what encouraged him to give his daughter to this one in marriage.

In short, the Divine Providence had penetrated his *Nasmah* (animal spirit). This was the reason why Isaiah chose him for conveying the message of God, but unfortunately he showed cowardliness against fighting with the powerful and the tyrannical. He disliked the order of the prophet, because his mind disliked it, and not that it was to the dislike of his reason as well. As a result of it, his mind was covered with a thick colour of disobedience for which God punished him in this way that his wife strayed away from the road, the wave swept away one of his two sons, and the remaining one was taken away by a wolf. He was very much grieved at this, repented to God, gave up comfortable living and continued to train himself for carrying the missionary work.

When he came to the people, he invited them to the oneness of God, but they, in turn, held him a liar, put him into prison and tortured him. He, therefore, prayed to God with all his devotion for their destruction, while the time of their destruction had not come as yet. God does not like to destroy a people until and unless the curse upon them has encompassed them from every side. Then his mind assumed an aspect similar to one acquired at the committing of murder without any right. God looked at them while he was in that aspect with the result that destruction came upon them and they were finished. Many happenings happened to him. Some of them are as under:

(1) When the people saw the punishment, they all repented to God and made entreaties to Him. God forgave them and averted

the punishment from them. There the devil deluded Jonah making him think that the people held him a liar and had firmly decided to harm him. He, therefore, became afraid of them and ran away from them without having besought God. As far as the perfect persons are concerned, it befits them to entrust their affairs to God. When they find that His Administration (*Tadbīr*) has penetrated all the worldly means, they begin to follow them accordingly.

(2) When he fled away, his mind assumed a different aspect. He embarked in a boat, and the waves came into agitation. He drew lots and, as a result of it, became of those cast away. He threw himself in the sea and then the fish took him into its mouth. Seeing this he glorified God, and asked for the forgiveness of his sin. God, then, forgave him and the Divine Mercy returned to him. He was thrown out by the fish on a naked shore while he was sick. God caused a gourd to grow for him, in order that the flies may not sit on him. It also occurred to the minds of animals to suckle him, as He made them think of him as their young one. Thus, compassion became excited in their hearts as it gets excited for their real young ones. This is how God became responsible for his affairs till he grew strong and healthy.

(3) The gourd tree then dried and that gazelle which used to give him suck also went away. He became very much grieved at this. God revealed to him saying, "O Jonah, you are weeping over a gourd which you never watered, and over a gazelle you never provided her with subsistence, but you do not weep over a lakh or even more."[5] This revelation, however, was the manifestation of some fault he had committed.

It is like this that when a pure person commits a fault, an ugly effect is left on his mind. Then it becomes necessary that he should understand that effect and also know that it is hated by God, either through a dream or through some external happening or through some Divine revelation, as it happens in the case of a person in the Intermediary World (*al-Barzakh*) when his

5. Qur'ān, xxxvii. 147 : "And We sent him to a **hundred thousand** or more."

mind would be in a state of tranquillity.

(4) Jonah once passed by a people who were gathering their fruits and then throwing them on the ground. He said to them, "Why are you spoiling your fruits and are taking no care of them?" God made a revelation to him saying, "You show anxiety about the fruits of these people, but you did not show any anxiety about a lakh or even more."[6]

(5) One day a man, who was a potter entertained him as a guest. God revealed to him saying, "Ask this man to break his pottery." When he asked him to do so, he (potter) abused him and said, "I find you mad." God thereby had set an example about his intention for his people.

(6) Once Jonah prayed to God to bless the cultivation of a certain person. He caused it to grow with the best growth, but in the end destroyed it. He became grieved at that, while, as a matter of fact, God had set a simile by it. He then made entreaties to God and asked for forgiveness. He forgave him and became responsible for his affairs as before.

(7) He restored his wife back to him, gave him one hundred dīnārs, and restituted his children to him. In addition to these favours, He brought him out of the belly of the fish, showed him some of His signs and assigned to him a true renown among his people.

God is like the mirror, as He had said, "Verily these are only your own actions which I count upon you."[7] Whosoever did a good work, he would be rewarded with good, and whosoever did an evil would be rewarded with an evil. The hearts of men are in His fingers. When He intends to punish a servant, He turns the hearts (of people) to what harms him, and when He intends to show favour to a person, He turns their hearts to where lies his good. This has always been the Divine course, especially in the case of those who are devoted to His command, and about whose education God had taken responsibility upon Himself; and Jonah was undoubtedly one of them.

6. Ibid.

7. Qur'ān, xviii. 49.

ZAKARĪYĀ, MARY, YAHYĀ AND JESUS

Ḥannah was an old barren woman. Once when she saw a pigeon feeding its chick with its bill, she longed for a child. She wept and made entreaties to God. He in return blessed that observation, that intense longing, and removed her barrenness and restored her young age to her. That happened in a way the physicians have mentioned, that with the observation of the male animal's mounting its female the mind wakes up to regain the procreative powers and the impotent becomes potent. Similarly, when she (Ḥannah) saw the pigeon feeding its chick, she remembered the matter of child and yearned for it very eagerly with the result that her abnormalities turned into normalities.

She was then inspired with the desire for a male child. Consequently, her imaginative faculty, her firm purpose and the soundness of her hope left a deep impression upon her embryo with the result that it became the blessed Mary. Her bodily constitution (*mizāj*) was like that of the male. Thus, she grew up strong in body, perfect in constitution, sound of nature (*fiṭrah*) and purity after the type of great men. It is, therefore, that the Holy Prophet has said: "Many men became perfect. . . ."[1] She was a female but possessed the qualities of the male, the reason being that by nature she was devoted to God and cherished hopes in Him alone. Her concentration joined her devotion and hope until they unitedly penetrated the faculty that shapes the child in the mother's womb.

When she gave birth to a female, she expressed her grief to God, as none happens to be free (*muḥarrar*) but the males, but God accepted Mary for His service in particular as she was a blessed lady with manly qualities. He then inspired Zakarīyā and

1. Bukhārī : "Many men became perfect but among women none became perfect except Āsiyah, wife of the Pharaoh, and Mary, daughter of 'Imrān : while 'Ā'ishah (Prophet's wife) is superior to all the other women as the soup (*tharīd*) is superior to all other foods.

other keepers of the Temple to accept her even though it went against the usual practice (according to which only the males were accepted for this service). God had bestowed many favours upon Mary. Some of them are as follows:

(1) He did not appoint any but Zakarīyā to look after her, as he was a prophet, a learned man and very kind and affectionate to her, and his wife was her step-mother. He also inspired the keepers of the Temple and the learned to decide as to who should be in charge of Mary by throwing (their) pens in the river. Every, one was under the impression that the matter will go in his favour, while, as a matter of fact, there was a cause in that pointing out the appearance of the truth in favour of Zakarīyā.

(2) God showed many signs to Mary. He created fruits for her with the word "*Kun*" (Be) without any elemental cause, as He would create them in the Paradise for its inmates.

Zakarīyā was a gnostic, the knower of His course (working) in His creation. He, however, came to know that the spiritual powers were to make a wonderful appearance in those days, and the creation those days did not depend upon an elemental cause, and those days were like the days when Adam was created. He, therefore, humbly prayed to God for the grant of a child who might succeed him, might establish religious teaching and invite people to the obedience of God: because he was afraid lest the children of his paternal uncles might take to the frail goods of this worldly life, and, thus, go astray and make others lose the right path as well. He, then, importunately prayed to God, Who readily accepted his prayer, made him young and removed the barrenness of his wife. As a consequence, Yaḥyā was born, who was wise, devoted to God and had kept himself away from the society of women.

The reason is that a thing for which the earthly causes do not take place suffers some weakness according to the animal characteristics, and becomes deprived of the comforts of life, even though it may be blessed in achieving the Divine nearness. The indifference (*zuhd*) of Yaḥyā and Jesus and their love for obscurity, their diversion from rulership and the sweet things of the world were the result of it. It is so because human perfection will not appear in a person but according to the natural capability of the *Nasmah* (animal spirit). Some persons turn out to be intelligent and their perfection lies in wisdom and firmness in knowledge. Others happen to possess a special taste for justice and politics, and they then pay their attention to God and are in turn given rulership.

Zakarīyā asked for a sign giving proof of the pregnancy of his wife with a child about whom good news had been given to him. God revealed to him saying: "You will not be able to speak with people for three days,"[2] the reason being that when the Providence of the Real (*al-Ḥaqq*) and the concentration of the Sublime Assembly descended upon this world, turning towards him, he was encompassed by an angelic state and, thus, could not speak but make only light hints.

Mary menstruated during the days the spiritual powers had penetrated that spot of land. When she became pure of menstruation, she withdrew to a place away from people for taking the bath. The time she let the curtain down and put off her clothes, God sent Gabriel to her in the form of a young, beautiful man, of complete make, full with bloom. Mary saw him while she was also young and constitutionally strong. She, therefore, became afraid of corruption and sought the protection of God sincerely, so that He might protect her. Mary's condition at that time was rather wonderful.

As for her nature (*ṭabī'ah*), it acquired what is always acquired during the intercourse, namely, the excitation of the procreative powers, just as a mere look (at the fair and full-grown) at times becomes the cause of seminal effusion. As regards her mind (*nafs*), it acquired protection of God and refuge with Him, till it became filled with the state of protection, poured down from the Unseen. As for the human form, it was, because of the association of Gabriel, at the top of making appearance.

When Gabriel told her: "I am the messenger of your Lord and have come to give you a pure male child,"[3] she became delighted, cheerful and pleased. Seeing her in that condition he (Gabriel) puffed into her vulva. The puffing caused tickling in her womb

2. Qur'án, xix. 10.

3. Qur'an, xix. 19.

with the result that she effused semen. As there was the potentiality of the semen of the male in her semen she became pregnant. Her seeking the protection of God, taking refuge with Him, her delight and her cheerfulness at the (presence of the) angelic state which dominated her, penetrated her embryo. Consequently, that state of her penetrated throughout the powers of her mind (*nafs*) including the power that shapes the child in the womb of the mother and the one which procreates.

This matter is like what the physicians have said, that he who desires to have a male child should think of him during the sexual intercourse. Then the predication (*ḥukm*) of the Similitudinary World and the attributes of Gabriel, through his puffing, penetrated the womb, as he was the cause of shaping the child. She (Mary), on that account, acquired in her nature a firm quality resembling that of Gabriel. This is the meaning of God's strengthening him (Jesus) through the Holy Spirit (Gabriel).

When Mary gave birth to Jesus, God showed many signs to her. Some of those signs are as follows:

(1) The angels informed her of all the perfections God was to bless her son with, and she also came to know of his conditions and perfections in general at the time of his childhood, young age and when he became full-grown.

(2) When she took refuge under a dry palm-tree, life penetrated it, and then it became green and bore fruit in a very short time, and God caused a spring to gush out for her.

(3) The time she was falsely accused of adultery, God averted that foul accusation from her by making the child (Jesus) to speak when it was not his time to speak. This became possible, because the spiritual powers were concealed in him.

When Jesus grew young, he was given the knowledge, the Book and the wisdom without any education, and many signs appeared in him. Some of them are as under:

(1) He used to tell people what they were eating and what they were storing up in the houses.

(2) He used to make the form of a bird from clay, then puffed into it and it became a living bird with the command of God. The life returned to it when his puffing penetrated the clay. This

transformation, thus, moved between puffing and life. Then after a short while it was falling dead.

(3) He brought the dead to life with the command of God, the reason being that the connection of the soul with the body is an imaginary one and not that of life. When Jesus prayed to God, He blessed that soul, the reflection of life fell on the dead and then it turned alive. As soon as he (Jesus) separated from it, it died then and there.

There were many a facility of life in the religion of Jesus. He made certain things lawful for his people which were previously forbidden. The reason is that the hard laws are prescribed only when the angelic faculty is to strike hard against the bestial one.

Jesus was just like an angel walking on the earth. The Jews accused him of sanctimony and decided to kill him. They contrived a device and God did the same, and He is the best in contriving a device. He made a similitudinary form of him, lifted him to the Heaven and cast his form on one of his followers or on someone from his enemies. That person was then killed under the impression that he was Jesus. God then helped his followers against their enemies with the result that they became victorious.

THE HOLY PROPHET MUHAMMAD

The principles of his sciences are many. Some of them are as follows:

(1) There was a natural relation between him and the Sublime Assembly (*al-Mala'-al-A'lā*), because his Rational Soul (*Nafs Nāṭiqah*) was sublime and his Nasmic Constitution was complete and balanced, necessitating the emergence of the excellent character. Besides, their (of Rational Soul and Nasmic Constitution) combination was based on their reconciliation. All this made it necessary that his heart should be continuously strengthened by them (Sublime Assembly). That strengthening, sometimes, assumed the form of their showing themselves to him; at times, they used to address him and inspire into his heart; and on certain occasions, he himself was seeing them in his sleep. An example of it is like that of a brave man who is perfect in bravery. He is excited by his temper of bravery moment after moment at the slightest cause towards fight with the enemy and towards rush into the warfare. Similarly, every temper has its relation to its consequences. On that account, whenever he (the Holy Prophet) was thoroughly strengthened by them in his wakefulness or sleep, many blessings of God, according to the causes that had encompassed him, were poured on him (from them).

On account of this quality, he was deliberately inclined to them, and remained encompassed by their blessings all the time, whether that time was a time when he was busy in the fight or a time when he was praying in seclusion in the mosque. Many of his miracles, such as the increase in the quantity of food and water were the result of this quality.

The reason of it is this that when a mind which happens to be an image of their support strongly concentrates upon a thing, then unavoidably a wide road from their concentration is also opened up. Their concentration subjugates this world of the three kingdoms of Nature (mineral, vegetable and animal) through inspiration, transformation and by occasioning the cause.

If it is their intention to produce fire, for example, and there is no cause for that in the world, and if it is there, it is so weak that it is not able to become the cause of producing it, then their intention necessarily gives rise to its (fire's) production. Judge the inspirations in the same way.

And because of this quality, his breast was split up and then filled with wisdom and faith. He was once taken to Jerusalem at night, from there to the Heavens and then to where God pleased. There he saw the souls of the prophets and had seen the angels in their real form and shape. He, then, reached the form of the Real, present in the heart of the Great Man (*Insān A'ẓam* = origin of humanity), and there he appeared in the most beautiful shape.

(2) He, on account of his nature (*fiṭrah*) God had created him upon, deserved to receive from the Sublime Assembly the knowledge of the purification of mind. That was because he possessed a sublime mind, complete *Nasmah* and was of a balanced constitution. He found that the various kinds of the deeds of piety depend upon the four cardinal virtues and the different kinds of the deeds of impiety depend on going against them. He was much grieved at those deeds which went against them, just as he who, when he feels hungry and thirsty, desires food and drink is grieved at their non-availability.

He then became devoted to the manifestation of their (of the four cardinal virtues) consequences just as the brave becomes devoted to the manifestation of the consequences of bravery; and just as the man who, by his very nature, is just becomes devoted to the administration of the town and the maintenance of the household economy. To this refers the Word of God: "And We revealed to them the doing of good actions."[1]

The Holy Prophet thought over the actions of virtue and vice which were in practice in those days, and then came to the conclusion that the origin of both is the spiritual state and they exercise an influence upon the purification and corruption of the mind. He also came to know as to how the actions of virtue increase in the realisation of the desired state and how the actions of vice

1. Qur'ān, xxi. 73.

increase in the realisation of the undesired state.

He also understood the occasion of every action and the weight of every thing; and understood how actions alone lead to happiness and unhappiness in the life after death. Besides, he understood how good actions are to be approached, and how evil ones are to be avoided. All the sciences pertaining to the forms of actions, the ways and means which were to perfect them (actions) and those causes which encourage people towards them gushed out of his thinking in the mirror of his mind, through his intuition and analogical deduction.

(3) God gave him intelligence by which he understood *Irtifāqāt*, namely, the ways of living, the maintenance of the household economy, the dealings, the administration of the town and of the nation. In addition, he became aware of the improvements which should be brought about among the people. Apart from that, he came to know of what is sound and what is unsound and what suits the universal considerations (*ārā'un kullīyun*) coming down from the side of the Truth (God). He also came to know of the particular considerations originating from the suggestions of the minds, and understood the causes for the injustice of the chiefs and the rulers and so on.

His example is like the example of the jurist (*Faqīh*) who ponders over the problems of his masters (*Mashā'ikh*) and then understands the cause of everything, comprehends the universal matters which they had in view and knows the valid and the invalid. And his example is like that of the wise and just ruler, who knows the course of the rulers who had gone before him, the reforms which they had in mind, knows the means and the causes and knows how to stop the thing from having its way by stopping its means.

If you were to think over the history of the rulers, you will be able to see that when one of them intended to lower the prices, he found that the cause of the rising of prices was either the paucity of the cultivators or the shortage of the traders. He then tried to remove the cause and by it achieved the desired object And if he intended to remain safe and secure against the mischief of the people, he commanded them not to ride the horses and not to take up arms. Again, when he intended that his supporters might not do wrong to him, he prohibited them from getting related by marriage among themselves, and that they should not pay visit to one another without the permission of the ruler, and so on. Such examples are, however, beyond number. In this way, the problems of politics are inferred and understood.

(4) God, out of His sheer kindness to His servants, intended that He might cause a spring of His mercy to gush out among men, where all might arrive, both the Arabs and the non-Arabs, to quench their terrible thirst, the reason being that the Arabs as well as the non-Arabs were following corrupt practices which were repugnant to the fair social and economic order and had turned their backs on their religious duties. They were the most ignorant of the creatures of God as to the purification of the minds, the most forgetful to the remembrance of the Hereafter, and the most negligent of the greatness and oneness of God. They were the devout worshippers of idols and devils, were most unjust towards the weak, and were the most reckless in cutting the connections of relationship.

God's kindness to them was that they might be awakened towards the danger they were in, might be led to the truth and made to follow the straight path, whether they liked it or not. This kindness was one of the affairs of the Administration (*Tadbīr*).

The Administration is the remainder of the Creation (*Khalq*), while the Creation is the remainder of the Origination (*Ibdā'*), the reason being that when God originated the Universal Soul, He originated it in such a form that it was capable of accepting every form. Sometimes, it was becoming a man, at times becoming a horse and, on certain occasions, appeared in the shape of a stone, etc.[2] Its being brought from power to action in these various states was, however, according to the requirements of the natural order

2. The self-unfolding Being, i.e. the Universal Soul, and the shadows bear some resemblance to the matter and the form respectively. On that account, the best of investigators (Shāh Walīyullāh) in some of his writings has called the self-unfolding Being and the shadows with these two names, the matter and the form respectively. He has said this by way of a metaphor and not by way of a reality. Refer : *'Abaqāt, 'Abaqah* 11, of Shāh Ismā'īl Shahīd.

which, by virtue of its being the remainder of its (Universal Soul's) origination, was good and fair (*khair*), and was according to the requirements of the Divine Grace which required Universal Soul's origination.

When the universe came into existence with all its particulars and every species and an individual acquired a form, requiring its particular characteristics, and when it was not fair to prevent the form from its characteristics nor was it fair to prevent the appearance of the events which were not inconsistent with the good order, it became necessary that He might raise causes in the earth and effect such changes as might bring the things to the best order. That was done in order to bring the creation to completion and perfection.

The example of the essential generosity in these three courses (creation, origination and administration) is like the example of a torrent which continues flowing on the surface of the earth until when it is pressed against by a dam, its water passes through its (dam's) cracks. From one crack it comes out in the form of a triangle, from the other in the shape of a square and from the third one in the form of a circle. Again, when another dam harder than the first one presses against it, the moisture and dampness penetrate the pores of the earth and the air. In this way, the effect of water reaches the other side of the dam.

In short, God's intention was then represented in the Sublime Assembly and there it assumed the form of a similitudinary person. This we name as the prophet of the prophets, and an origin of the Divine Signs. From there the drops of mercy fell on the earth and the springs of kindness gushed out from the root of the three kingdoms of Nature in every age and period according to the requirements of the events taking place in those times. In certain periods, those drops of mercy fell on the hearts of the children of Adam and they were the apostles and the prophets. But this affair was not to become complete here until there might be found such matter in the order (*niẓām*) of the earth as may be fit for drawing the picture of that form as the picture of man is drawn in the mirror. The pictured form of man here is that intention of God represented in the Sublime Assembly, while the mirror is a man from the children of Adam who disputes with the enemies of truth, fights with them, generously spends away his wealth and tries to bring unity among people. This, however, he will do as the rulers of the people do (sometimes through peaceful means and at times through use of force).

By the drawing of his picture is meant that his actions may be puffed into by the Holy Spirit *(Rūḥ Qudsī)*, and by it is meant that intention which is represented in the Sublime Assembly.

The requirement (*māddah*) of this age was the Holy Prophet himself. The springs of Divine Law then gushed out from there, followed by suitable adjustments, namely, the fixation of the quantities so that the people may not be obliged to follow but what is accurate, which may not allow any change and suffer any disorder by the passage of time. Again, it (Law) should be like a perceptible thing, current among the people, and to which they stick in their seeking the nearness of God. He, therefore, revealed the glorious Qur'ān, prescribed for them the circumambulation of the Ancient House (Ka'bah) and commanded them to follow the Divine Law. The revelation of the Qur'ān was fixed in the Arabic language (mother tongue of the Arabs) and the circumambulation of that House was prescribed which they used to circumambulate from centuries. Besides, only those laws were prescribed which were in vogue among the people who followed the religion of Ismā'īl and Isaac (Isḥāq). To this fact, the Word of God makes reference: "He has not made any hardship for you in the religion; **it is the same religion that has come down to you from your father Abraham."**[3]

God then poured Islam into the hearts of his chosen Companions with the result that the incentive for *Jihād* (Holy War) spread in their breasts as the air spreads in the skin bag at the **time of puffing. Thus, they became "a community raised for the people"**[4] **to invite them to the right path. The Divine Mercy came** to defend and protect them, until the command of God came for execution, and Islam entered into every house of the town and village, in spite of the weakness of the weak and the power of the powerful.

3. Qur'ān, xxii. 78.

4. Qur'ān, iii. 110.

(5) His pure self (*nafs*) was fit that the past and the future events of the world might be disclosed to it, the reason being that the universal events with their similitudinary forms assume large shapes in the Sublime Assembly, while the particular events which are the result of the weak causes and do not influence the Sublime Assembly, willingly or unwillingly, do not assume a large shape, but only when the time of their appearance draws near.

As regards the future events, there are, however, certain causes for them, and those causes again have some other causes behind and so on. When the natural order (*niẓām*) comes to a few of the causes, the generosity and the mercy of God make it necessary that the forms of the events occasioned by them (causes) may appear in some shape in the perceptive faculties of the Sublime Assembly. As the causes multiply and the time of their appearance approaches nigh, the larger and faster becomes their assumed form.

The secret of all this is that the knowledge of the natural order (*niẓām ṭabī'ī*) which is a particular form of the Universal Soul is a higher science. The most pure, however, deserves that the picture of the event may appear drawn before him in its very beginning, but the one who is lower than him in purity; it, however, appears drawn before him rather later. This picture of the events appears sooner or later according to the purity of the person.

As regards the past events, it may be remembered that the forms of men are suspended in the Holy Fold. This we have known through vision. When a man does a good action, his mind becomes perfect, the Sublime Assembly becomes pleased, and God, on that account, shows mercy to him. Brightness and light appear in his form and a white mark is left on it. But if he does an evil action, his mind corrupts, the Sublime Assembly is displeased, and God, on account of that, curses him. The darkness and blackness appear in his form, and a black mark is left on it. This form, however, continues to remain there in the Holy Fold until the time of the end of this turn comes. As soon as that turn is over, the forms disappear. When any gnostic joined it (the Holy Fold), the conditions of people in relation to their forms were disclosed to him as God pleased. To some, only a part of this disclosure is made and to some a considerable portion of it, according to their ranks before God. A part of our speech in connection with ancient prophets and holy persons is of this kind.

Sometimes, the form of a great event which is to take place for doing a great favour to people or for a widespread destruction is firmly fixed in the perceptive faculties of the Sublime Assembly, which, however, a gnostic knows and understands from there. At times, when the gnostic hears some news people were talking about out of their carelessness and ignorance, he derives through the interpretation of that news what goes to separate the right from the wrong, and is then led to the truth conforming to the event.

In short, it rarely happens that one who joined the Sublime Assembly entered into their fold but did not get the picture of those great events drawn on the plate of his mind according to the original constitution he was created upon.

Now when his (Holy Prophet's) pure self implied the domination of the world and the leadership of religion, and had strongly participated with the Sublime Assembly in the great works of the Administration, it became necessary that the picture of the stories of the ancients and that of the general events which bore relation to religion with regard to its propagation or the neglect thereof be drawn in it (in the self of the Prophet). And also the picture of that event or story, etc., which may be the requirement of the natural order in man or it may be from the requirements of the great cause and so on may be portrayed in his mind.

The events which are to take place before the Resurrection, such as the appearance of the Antichrist, of Imām Mahdī, the descending of Jesus, the emergence of the beast of the earth (*Dābbat al-Arḍ*) and the coming out of Gog and Magog, are the greatest general events in assuming the form, because their cause is the natural order. The detailed account of this all is that the cause of the appearance of the Resurrection and its signs has recourse to three things and they are as follows :

(1) The earthly and the heavenly causes will give rise to the such as the conquest of Iraq, Syria and Egypt, and the acquisi-

and much of the vegetable and the mineral, such as the swallowing up by the earth, the countless number of deaths, the earthquakes, the roarings and the quarrels and strifes (among people).

(2) The corrupt aspects will rise from the earth, some from the actions of people performed intentionally and some from such matters as they had no choice in them whatsoever. The atmosphere will, thus, assume the form of those corrupt aspects. Naturally, the generosity of God will not descend but coloured with those corrupt aspects. The world would then be prepared for the appearance of such persons who, because of their excess and extravagance, will be far removed from the limits God had fixed for the species of man.

Some of them will incline to abstraction and others will incline to bestiality. Thereafter, a disease will set in the species of man itself. Other aspects more hateful and stinking than them (first ones) will arise. The generosity of God will descend coloured with them. The world will be prepared for the appearance of such men as will be far removed from the first state, and so on. Time would come when analogical deductions will go wrong. No astrologer will be trusted in his astrology and no physicist will be relied upon in his physics. Goodness will completely disappear and no one would be found in the earth to remember God. Many events will happen or will be made to take place on account of certain unexpected causes, such as the prayers (made by people) and the attention (paid by them) towards the spirits, etc. At that time, it will become necessary to break the then existing order (*naẓm*).

(3) There is a hidden secret implied in the Divine Wisdom which cannot be questioned as to "why" and "how," just as it cannot be questioned as to why the fire is hot and dry unlike water, and as to why the sun travels from the east to the west in its one kind of movement and from the west to the east in its other kind of movement.

Then after that, the events which took place in the Community and the Caliphate had assumed a very large shape, particularly those events which happened in the days of the Orthodox Caliphs, such as the conquest of Iraq, Syria and Egypt, and the acquisition of the abundance of wealth and the events which led to the destruction of Chosroes after whom no other Chosroes arose and the destruction of Caesar after whom no other Caesar ever appeared. In addition to these, you take into account the events which took place during the unjust rule of Banū Umayyah as these events had assumed a bold form, and the events which took place in the days of the Abbasid Caliphate, followed by the civil wars of the Saljūq Turks, the Chingīz and others.

These assumed forms are, however, of various degrees and ranks. When any assumed form is compared with one bolder than that, it appears insignificant, and the man then speaks of it in the strict sense, for example, a man who does not know the affair, as it actually is, begins to think of it contrary and repugnant to that. An example of that is the saying of the Holy Prophet: "His country is Syria." Now here he said these words strictly speaking. This caused confusion in the mind of someone that, besides Syria, there are other countries as well, which are most vast and prosperous. But the truth is that he (the Holy Prophet) looked at the form which was in the second rank and gave information of it, as if the form which was in the third rank was no form at all to deserve mention.

Similarly, he said: "This religion will continue to dominate until there appear twelve caliphs."[5] Here one begins to doubt that if by it the Prophet meant the caliphate of the prophethood, then it surely ended with the end of the thirty years and with the rule of the first four Caliphs, but if by it he meant the rule of justice and righteousness, then these qualities were found in a better form in some of those who came after them as well. Again, if he meant the twelve caliphs coming one after another in the irregular order, even then the number of the just and the righteous was rather greater.

In fact, the decline and the change do come in the nation by degrees. What was found in the days of the first four Caliphs was not seen in the days of others. Similarly, what was seen in the days of the Syrian rule was not found after it. The Prophet reckoned

5. *Sunan Abū Dāwūd*, Vol. II : "Kitāb al-Mahdī".

only those two ranks and did not take much care of what followed them. Thus, both the ranks became complete with (the rule of) the twelve caliphs, who, all of them, were from the Quraish. They are as under: The first four Caliphs, Mu'āwiyah, 'Abdullāh b. Zubair, 'Abd-ul-Malik, his four sons, and 'Umar b. 'Abd-ul-Azīz. Then happened what happened.

Similarly, there are his sayings about the approach of Resurrection. He has informed that he had been raised before it, as if, he thereby did not reckon the events and the duration of time that preceded it.

The light which we have named before as the prophet of the prophets deserved to become an instrument of the Real (*al-Ḥaqq*) for the descent of His mercy in particular, which may lead to completely cover the minds of the disobedients with mercy, change their evil deeds into good ones and remove away the filth of the worldly, mean forms with which their minds were stained.

The cause of his becoming the instrument of the Real on that day was the Divine Grace, which in our days became the cause of the descent of the Laws, the raising of the prophets and the fixation of the signs of God on earth. That however, depends upon the strong and continuous ambition of a man, perfect in the proper sense of the word, so that his ambition may become like the mould for the ingot of gold, and like the nest for the bird or like the form for an undefined matter.

His example is like that of the Universal Soul, which does not come down to the earth, nor does it become manifest in the three kingdoms of Nature, nor does it get fixed in the particular moulds but only when the earth is found fit for that, and some great Divine favours so require. This is why the semen of the father and the womb of the mother are a condition for the flow of the human soul, and the penetration of air and water in the earth and the throwing of the seed in it are a condition for the flow of the vegetable soul. Judge other things in like manner.

God had already decided that that man should be Muḥammad, who will make a very strong desire on that (Judgment) Day before his Lord with the result that His generosity will flow in abundance, in due regard to his being the prophet of the prophets. This secret remained concealed in his mind, which he came to know of when he understood his own self (*nafs*). That generosity made it necessary that he might have the knowledge of the events of the Judgment Day and it also necessitated his superioriy to the whole of mankind. Besides, he came to know that all the people including Adam and others below him in the rank would come under the shadow of his banner, and that he would make the greatest intercession. And that man would be the most fortunate of the people in winning the blessing of his intercession who for his bearing love for him and invoking the blessings of God upon him frequently had acquired the capability for receiving it. Thus, from this perfection of his, four sciences sprang up, and they are as under:

(1) The science of the Reckoning. The reality of it is that the people on that Day will come to know of the actions which had stuck to the roots of their hearts and will have the information of those good and bad actions which had become imprinted on them (their hearts). Besides, they will have the knowledge of the property of every action which prepares man for punishment or reward. They will come to know of all these realities on that Day, as the thick worldly curtains of darkness will be removed from them. The Reckoning is meant for that Day only because of a fact (*amr*) which refers to them. As for the Reckoning from God, it is always there and needs no renewal.

However, when the time of Reckoning will come, the Divine Grace will make it necessary that certain (similitudinary) bodies may appear in which the spirit of the Reckoning may be infused and in which (bodies) the nature (*mizāj*) of the Great Man (*Insān Akbar*) particularises, just as the nature of the Small Man (*Insān Asghar*) particularises in its perceptive faculties the appearance of cowardliness in the form of a rabbit and that of anger in the shape of a lion.

There are certain principles of the bodies which have been clearly explained by the Prophet. And they are as under:

(*i*) The actions will be presented and they will assume a suitable, substantial form bearing some kind of resemblance to the actions done. The Prophet has explained that a large scald-headed snake will be put round the neck of a man who did not pay the poor-rate (*Zakāt*), or he will be trodden by the camel with its feet, or he will be gored by the bull. Similarly, he has explained what kind of punishment will be given to the usurper and the defrauder. About the treacherous he has said that a banner will be hoisted by the side of his buttocks. God has said: "Their light will be running before them."[6] Or the actions will assume an accidental form like the whiteness and the blackness of the faces and the tallness of the neck of the crier to prayer (*Mu'adhdhin*) and so on.

(*ii*) The reading of the Scrolls, their being given to men from the right, from the left and from behind the backs, and the conversation of God with them in His words: "Had I not made you the chief (to be obeyed) and authorised you to receive one-fourth of the booty?"[7]

(*iii*) Every community will be ordered to follow its deity which will hurl it down into the fire of Hell. The believers, however, will be delivered by a particular manifestation (*tajallī*) they will have a claim to, because of their correct faith in God and in His attributes.

(*iv*) The Balance will be set up and actions will be weighed including that letter which contained the words "There is no god but Allah."

(*v*) The appearance of the hidden good qualities which had not assumed a larger shape by their actions done in the world in this way that God commanded a servant to do something which he did, and from it appeared his obedience to Him and his hope in Him; and the other cases of such kind.

(*vi*) The Bridge will be erected over the Hell, and the prongs of fire will appear. Some men will cross it like the lightning, or like the wind, or like the swift-running horse. Some will pass over it safely by walking. Others will cross it receiving many a scratch. There would be some among them who would be caught in the fiery prongs and will thus fall into the fire. All these are the forms of the Reckoning by God (*al-Ḥaqq*) and of the people's coming to

6. Qur'ān, lvii. 12.

7. *Nihāyah Fī Gharīb al-Ḥadīth*, Vol. II.

know of their actions.

(2) The science of the descent of mercy from the side of the prophet of the prophets. Its reality has already been explained by us. It will be represented in many forms.

One of them is that on that Day the intercession of the prophets, the apostles, the saints (*auliyā'*), the Qur'ān and the actions will take place. The prophets and their companions who died as martyrs will contend with the rebellious unbelievers, laugh at them and will rejoice at their suffering.

The other one is the appearance of the Fountain. From it only the sincere believers will drink and the rest will be driven away as the stranger camel is driven away from the watering-place.

(3) The science pertaining to the suitable, substantial or accidental forms which the ease and difficulty will assume there.

It may be remembered that the human spirit, so long as it is in the world, goes not progressing and enjoying a delicate life in many ways. All the human beings without exception are participating in those ways of enjoyment, such as to have delicious food, palatable drink, charming wife, splendid garments and fine residence, etc. However, there are certain enjoyments which are peculiar to some only. It is, therefore, that the Holy Prophet has said that God has created a brown, red-lipped girl for Ja'far, as He knew the liking of Ja'far for such a kind of girl Similar are his sayings in connection with the camel and the horse, etc.[8]

Every condition of ease and comfort which represents delight, cheerfulness and satisfaction in our sleep will surely be the lot of the believer in the Paradise. And every state of difficulty and suffering which is represented by hatred, loneliness and the unsettlement of mind will be the lot of the unbeliever and the hypocrite in Hell-fire. These are some words spoken in the general form, but they have been very clearly explained by the Holy Prophet.

(4) God will manifest Himself to them on an elevated spot in the Paradise. This favour will not be shown to them in conse-

8. *Sunan Tirmidhi* : "*Abwāb Ṣifat al-Jannat*".

quence of their actions, but they will receive it as a purely God-given and natural favour outside their acquisition, the reason being that the (Great) Human Soul (*an-Nafs-ul-Insānīyah*) will puff into them, and because they had been created in the best form. No doubt, actions remove the obstructions and lift the curtains. It is, therefore, that the Holy Prophet has said: "Surely you will see your Lord clearly just as you see the moon. Thus, whosoever among you is able to observe prayer before the rising of the sun and the one before its setting, then let him do that."[9]

It may be remembered that the Holy Prophet has not allowed us to think over the person (*Dhāt*) of God, but, on the contrary, he has prohibited us from that, as he has said: "Do not think over the person of God"; "There should be no thinking over God." His prohibition includes discussion on the attributes of God as well, namely, the explanation of the realities of His attributes and the way He is characterised by them, such as whether the seeing and the hearing are other than the knowledge or the knowledge itself and whether the speech is personal or something else, and so on. However, there were certain things which the Holy Prophet found both the Arabs and the non-Arabs understanding them and characterising their Lord by them. For example, when they used to mention His greatness, sanctity, purity and power over the created beings, they were characterising Him by the administrative ability of the ruler, as he (the Holy Prophet) found that their perfection will not be complete but by their knowing them (the attributes of God) in this way, and saw that they had always been describing their Lord with these attributes from a very long time. Accordingly, he laid the foundation of his mission on reminding them of the days of adversity and prosperity God used to bring them by turns. While mentioning them (God's attributes) he used that language which they were using. He did not engage himself in giving an exposition of their realities and did not go deep in them. However, he could not prevent himself from the use of such similes as the hand, the

9. Ibid., "*Bāb Mā Jā'a Fī Rūyat al-Rabb.*"

foot and the laughing.

Many centuries known to their goodness passed away in this way. Then some people came who named themselves as Ahl al-Sunnah (the observers of the traditional law, Sunnites), while, as a matter of fact, the *Sunnah* (practice of the Prophet) was far away from them. They, thus, made forced attempts at what concerned them not, and at what their prophet had not brought. Oh! what a calamity, which became universal and which blinded the people!

There are certain principles for the miracles which appeared at the hands of our Prophet, and at the hands of the perfect men. Some of them are as follows:

(1) Luck. Its reality is that there is a certain point in the minds of men to which all other minds are attracted, and which subdues them all. It pulls them towards itself as the magnet pulls the pieces of iron to itself. If it happens to be extremely fortunate, it necessitates the flow of such thoughts in the mind of that person, in the minds of people around him and even in the minds of animals and angels, which bring ease and comfort to him. But, if it happens to be extremely wretched, it makes it necessary that such thoughts may flow in the mind of that person, in the minds of the people, animals and angels around him, which lead to his difficulty and distress.

I have seen many a time that whenever the destiny (*qaḍā'*) was to take place for the death of a certain man, for example, it flowed in search of the causes as water flows in the grassy ground or like the penetration of the rays of the sun through the rent curtain. It (destiny), however, takes into consideration the weight between the cause and the obstacle. If the grass and the straw are to prevent the free flow of water and the curtain prevents the penetration of the rays of the sun, then their flow and penetration will take practical shape as far as possible. In like manner, the destiny will flow according to the nearest cause available there. If there is some depression in the ground, and if its (destiny's) taking place there is not opposed to the natural order, then it will flow towards that man, and a thought will also occur to his mind to go near it (depressed ground) with the result that his foot will slip there and this will become the cause of his death. If there is his enemy and the appearance of enmity is also not opposed to the natural order, the destiny moves towards him, and there it occurs to the mind of his enemy to quarrel with him or he (the man) becomes angry and abuses the enemy with the result that the quarrel ends in his death. And if there is an animal, the destiny moves towards it with the result that it strikes him with its foot or bites him strongly and this brings about his death. But if the inspiration of the angels happens to be the nearest of the causes on that day, then the destiny will move towards them (angels) so that they may execute the order which was to be carried through anyhow. For these causes, however, there are certain other causes for everything, which unavoidably necessitate them, and luck is one of such necessary causes.

We have observed many a time that in the mind of a certain person there is a bright point like the brightly shining star, and the rays radiating from it penetrate the hearts of men, the angels and the animals. If they (the rays) are effective and the penetrated one is also receptive, then it will necessitate the emergence of an intention of doing good and showing love to him.

Sometimes, there is a point in the mind of a certain man, but it is not so bright and shining like the one mentioned above. That man then pays attention to the reading of the Divine Names and other litanies. As a result of it, that point begins to shine very brightly. On account of this, (Divine) mercy, affection and kindness were shown to the Holy Prophet from the time of his birth and when he was a nursling under his nurse. His friends were always helped, his enemies were defeated, and he was defended against every evil. In this state he went on progressing till he reached the highest stage.

(2) He was created in the best form and in a balanced constitution, at a time when there was an excellent combination of the powers of the stars which required a great renown and prevalence for him and his leadership of both the Arabs and the non-Arabs, to whom they might submit and obey. And they also demanded that his religion should continue until the Day of Judgment.

God has placed some effect and property in every kind of species, the individuals and the situations (*Auḍā'*). There is absolutely no opposition from the best order (*Niẓām khair*) to prevent a thing from its effect and property. Thus, this merit of his (namely, his inborn qualities) made it necessary that he should be the most beautiful and the most perfect of the people in creation, the most brave, the most generous, the most forbearing, the most just and the most eloquent of them. He grew up among the people who were the noblest of the Arabs and the best of people. Apart from the prophets, the hermits who followed them and the pious Arabs, the persons who possessed some particular kind of knowledge of the decisions taking place in the Holy Fold, such as the divines, the Jinn, the astrologers and some others had inferred from the knowledge and the information they possessed that all these things were meant for him.

These were the two qualities which are shared with him by just, fortunate and morally strong kings, according to their capability. It is rare that the extraordinary things of the sort we have mentioned should not have been related of him who happened to be perfect in his character, and at the time of whose birth fortunate powers had combined in the stars.

(3) He was intelligent, and, on account of the purity of his mind from all the stains which produce rust and which prevent it from getting imprinted by what takes place in the Holy Fold, he used to receive from the Unseen the news of the past events and those of the future as far as God liked. We have already made a mention of that secret.

Sometimes, certain things were represented to him in his dream and he came to know of their reality by means of an interpretation or even without any means. At times, no sooner some things without any colour or shape, etc., appeared to him in his wakefulness than they disappeared. On certain occasions. an angel (in the form of man) used to appear to him and address him, and he was then receiving the information from him into his mind. In cases like these, it is necessary for one to whom God has given the knowledge of the interpretation of the dreams to deeply think over two things and they are as under:

One is that this event should necessarily be distinguished from the other events, until it may appear distinctly separate from them, and for that there are many reasons. One of them is that there should be an obvious desire in the mind of man for that event, like that of the thirsty person for water or like the hidden desire in the mind of the poor for wealth and for such means of earning and devices which lead him to its acquisition, even though such thoughts may not occur to his mind at that moment.

The other one is the strong representation of the event which takes place in the Sublime Assembly. As a result of that, if there is a man who is inclined towards those events (taking place in the Sublime Assembly) to a certain extent in some form or the other, then unavoidably something from them gets imprinted on his mind. That generally happens when the great events take place such as the appearance of one government, the overthrow of the other and the widespread famines and epidemics, etc. This form of the events which appears in the Sublime Assembly invariably agrees with the dreams of the people and their visions.

The third reason is the Administration of God. Thus, the best order (*Niẓām khair*) does not become complete, but only when the knowledge is poured into the heart of one who is fit for that. It is, therefore, that the Pharaoh in particular saw famine in his dream so that he might be informed of it in advance.[10] The knowledge again is not poured into the heart of any but through two principles: one is the capability of the person concerned and the other is the generosity of God and the flow of His mercy. There are, however, certain reasons when these two principles combine. One is, where the generosity of God dominates the capability of the recipient. That happens in the case of such sciences on which depends the reformation of the masses or of a people or of an individual. The other is where the capability of the recipient happens to exceed the generosity of God. That takes place in the case of such sciences as do not relate to the reformation of the people.

The first one is the origin of the sciences of the prophets which are absolutely certain and it is proper that the people should be obliged to follow them. The second one is the origin of

10. This perhaps refers to the Pharaoh of Egypt, when the Prophet Joseph was put in the prison. He had seen a dream which was correctly interpreted by the Prophet as pointing out to the impending famine.

the sciences of the saints and they also happen to be true in relation to one state (*Ḥāl*) against the other and in relation to one individual against the other. However, there are exceptions in the case of those who happen to be the heirs of the prophets (as the disclosures made to them are generally certain, above equivocation).

The fourth reason is that the event should be bearing some relation to the mind of this person. There are persons whose nature is suitable for knowing the particular happenings, while there are some other persons whose nature is fit for knowing the great and universal affairs.

The other one is the freedom of the mind from its worldly connections.[11] This becomes the cause of many other secret causes. Some works lead to the comfort of the heart, and some others keep the mind always engaged. There are some ambitions which lead to deep thinking, and there are certain competitions which lead to sharp-mindedness.[12]

(4) He was graced with a great blessing in his person (*nafs*) and in all that had connection with it. The reality of the blessing is that a strong cause resulting from the blessings, the prayer and the pleasure of the Sublime Assembly turns to the servant, gets mixed up with his person and then leads to the expansion of the natural causes.

Ordinarily, there are some spiritual states which do not give rise to the feeling of hunger, nor do the parts of the body disintegrate on account of the natural heat, such as when one is busy in repelling the disease or is overtaken by shame, fear and impetuosity, etc. For that state there is a capability in the mind and the body of man.

When the blessing descends and meets with that capability it makes it necessary that the man may keep away from food for a longer time, even longer than what reason requires in that body. The blessed person, when he desires to manifest this effect, oftentimes, sticks to the recitation of the name of *aṣ-Ṣamad* (Lord) and

11. Connected with the words: "One is that this event" (p. 87).

12. In Shah Waliyullah Academy's edition the word is *Inhijām* (withdrawal), but *Ḥijā'* (sharp-mindedness) seems to be more appropriate.

al-Quddūs (Holy) and the like, in order to direct himself to this spiritual state and then the blessing will appear in that form.

Ordinarily, there are certain states which lead to the known violence and wakefulness, like the cheerfulness of the heart, the appearance of impetuosity, competition and fear, etc. There is a capability for those states as well. When the blessing descends and meets with this capability, it becomes necessary that his violence and wakefulness should increase manifold.

Many a time, a man sees certain acts and states in his companion, and from them he understands many of the hidden things, which, however, he is unable to find in the other state. For that state also, there is a capability. When the blessing meets with that capability, it necessitates the emergence of insight (*firāsah*), completely outside the ordinary course.

In every mind, there is a form of man's belief he has in his Lord and in His signs. Similarly, for every kind of belief with which his heart has a connection, there is the form of it. Sometimes, when man pays his fullest attention to that belief, it assumes many shapes and forms. That generally happens in sleep, and rarely takes place in wakefulness. At times, when the blessing descends on him and he also happens to possess that required capability, it (the blessing) necessitates the appearance of Divine Manifestations and correct dreams, which are, however, beyond the reach of a common man.

In short, one of the miracles (*Mu'jizāt*) of the Holy Prophet which are narrated without any break in the transmission-chain was that whenever he prayed for increase in food or drink, God brought abundance therein. That blessing took practical shape either in the increase of the quality of the thing only and, thus, it was proving more profitable, or in the increase in the quantity of the thing itself. The matter then yielding to the force of the concentration of the Sublime Assembly was assuming the form of water or food. For such things, there are examples even in (the phenomena of) Nature.

These are the two qualities which are shared with him by the most intelligent and the saints. It is, therefore, that you see the books of the persons of their rank replete with the various kinds of these miracles, such as intuition (*kashf*), advance information (*ishrāf*), hearing the Unseen Voice (*hātif*) and the acceptance of their prayers, etc.

Some happenings take place sparingly, because their causes take place but very sparingly. They are, therefore, named as extraordinary (*khawāriq*). As a matter of fact, all that is named as extraordinary is of the ordinary ones, but because their causes take place rarely, they appear but rarely; and as the people do not usually expect them, they are named as extraordinary.

At times even for the extraordinary thing, there is an example they are familiar with, and even for a thing which is more surprisingly extraordinary, but people do not pay attention to that. When any extraordinary thing appeals them the most, they begin to wonder at it, highly speak of it and write it in their history books. For example, when water turns into marble in a moment, they do not pay attention to it, but if it changes into some body they are not expecting, nor such a thing had ever been heard by them, they take it to be strange.[13]

Sometimes a thing is taken extraordinary in one species and not in the other such as deep insight, covering long distance in a short time, assumption of different forms and influencing the mind of the other person. Jinn are familiar with these works and people do not take them as strange. But if such a work is seen in a human being, they take it as extraordinary.

In short, some events take place, and God makes them as a miracle of one of His prophets in some way or the other. For example, the prophet gives information of the coming of an event before it actually takes place, or that event, when it happens, conforms to the punishment about which God had made a revelation to him. Just as God destroyed the 'Ād and the Thamūd on account of their disobedience, which (their disobedience) brought in its wake their destruction. Then God made that as a miracle of Heber and Ṣāliḥ.

Some scholars who possess the knowledge of the Tradition and the natural philosophy are of the view that the splitting of the

13. Qur'ān, xii. 105 : "And how many signs in the heaven and the earth do they pass by ? Yet they turn (their faces) away from them !"

moon is also one of such events, as it is an event which happens rarely. God has made it as a sign for the nearness of the Resurrection, just as He has made the swallowing up by the earth, the earthquakes and the great bloody wars as signs for it, and has made it (split of the moon) as a miracle for our Holy Prophet. When people asked him about its (Resurrection's) sign, he informed them that God will soon show them a sign. When the moon split up, he showed it to them.

These scholars are of the opinion that it is not necessary that the splitting of the moon should have taken place in the very body of the moon itself. It is rather possible that it should have been like the smoke, the falling of the stars, the eclipse of the sun and the moon, which appear to the eyes of people in the air. Then, for them, such words in the Arabic language were used which suited the substance of these things. It is, therefore, that the Holy Qur'ān was revealed in the language of the Arabs.

An example of it is provided by the saying of 'Abdullāh b. Mas'ūd, who is sufficient as an authority for that. He has narrated that whenever people were smitten by famine, they used to look around (in despair) and saw a smoke in the sky (while as a matter of fact there was no smoke). These words of God have been revealed in that connection: "The Day the sky will come with clear smoke."[14]

Ibn al-Mājishūn, who is one of the Imāms of guidance, has said that God on the Judgment Day will not change from one form to another form, but people will see Him in various forms. He has said that the cause of this event (namely, of the splitting of the moon) is that when the transparent constituents of water combine together and become like one single plane, and if at that time there happens to be a mountain or a thick cloud behind it, then it will become like the mirror in which the moon would be seen reflected. At that time, people will see two moons instead of one, in the air.

Sometimes, the thing reflected in the mirror is other than the one in the sky. At times, the whole moon becomes concealed and

14. Qur'ān, xliv. 10.

instead the halves appear in the air. An example of this all is like the example of the eclipse of the sun and the moon and the falling of the stars. It has come in the Qur'ān that they all are the Signs. I have said this much, by way of possibility and probability, while God otherwise is All-Powerful and the true knowledge is with Him alone.

You should know that the straight path in this problem and in the allegories such as the hands and the feet (of God) and in the matters of the future life is that man should follow their external meaning and should not busy himself in knowing the nature of their existence. He should generally believe that what God and His Prophet have intended by them is true, and should not say that God inended this and did not intend that, etc. It is, therefore, that you will never find the Holy Prophet, his Companions and the best of their followers having ever busied themselves in anything of that kind. This kind of business (namely, to know the allegorical) came from the Mu'tazilites, who had stolen this science from the philosophers. The Sunnites afterwards stole it from the Mu'tazilites. We have already made it thoroughly clear in some of our works, that the Mu'tazilites had stolen it from the philosophers, from whom (the Mu'tazilites) it was stolen by the Sunnites.

WONDERS OF THE WORLD

Here we draw your attention to certain principles of wonders which have taken place in the world.

You should know that, in our opinion, the whole universe is one body, with one soul connected with it, and with one order under which the soul rules its body. The example of all the happenings which are taking place in the four kingdoms of Nature, namely, the mineral, the vegetable, the animal and man, is like the example of the form reflected in the mirror. In the elements, it is only the form of the conjunction of the powers of the stars that is reflected and nothing else. Just as the form reflected in the mirror combines all the predications (*Aḥkām*) of both the things reflected and of the mirror, similarly the happenings taking place in the universe do combine the predications of the conjunctions of the stars as well as those of the elements.

In short, when man looks into any mirror, his form will be reflected in it and not that of the horse. All the parts of his body will be reflected in it, namely, his head, hands, feet, eyes, ears and the nose, etc., and not the form of the tail, the trunk, the crest of the cock, the horns and that of the cloven hoofs.

When something is put in front of the mirror, its exact form will be reflected in it. If the breadth of the mirror is greater than its length or its length is longer than its breadth or if it is triangular or is red or green, the thing reflected therein will assume the same variations accordingly. Thus, for every looker and the mirror there is a general predication and both of them (the looker and the mirror) conform to the particular reflection.

Similarly, it is proper here to consider the case of the happenings. No one can understand their realities until he has possessed a thorough knowledge of the science of the earthly natures, their properties, and has carefully watched them in the happenings. Where contraction and expansion were not found supported by the earthly causes, he may be able to prove the heavenly causes for them (happenings). He will not understand the realities of the happenings until he has comprehended the knowledge of the powers of the stars and their complete predication, which, however, deserves to take practical shape if there is no obstruction. He will find contraction and expansion there which will show him the need towards establishing the properties of the four kingdoms of Nature. Now, when you have become sure of what we have mentioned, it is time to mention one other cause.

It should be remembered that there is one other cause behind these two causes, emerging from the order under which the Universal Soul administers the Universal Body. Its example is like that of the man who possesses certain predications which are flowing from the human species, and which are present in all the human individuals in one and the same form. For example, every human individual must certainly be of a straight stature, clear in skin, with wider nails, laughing and speaking one. It is also necessary that he should be an embryo in the beginning, then a born one, then a child, then a boy, then a youth, then a full-grown, then an old one and then a decrepitude.

When he was a child, his constitution (*mizāj*) was fresh and his intellect was unripe. Again, when he became young, his constitution dried and his intellect became ripe. The time he turned old, weakness appeared in many of his faculties and the clear freshness dominated him. The male is more jealous than the female, is more brave and more intelligent, and so on. All these predications are flowing from the specific form. And the specific form is that which requires the penetration of the universal predication in all it makes its appearance. All that we have mentioned or have made a reference to is the explanation of this predication. It is, therefore, that there is a different predication for every species. No individual of the species remains behind its predication, save one the matter of which disobeys it at the very outset.

Similarly, the Primal Form, by that I mean, the Universal Soul *(an-Nafs al-Kullīyah)* has its own predication in its body, in its limbs and in its faculties from which it (predication) never remains blind. It is the requirement of that predication that whenever a human species, for example, is found and if a matter differing in its attributes accepts its form (form of human species), then it becomes necessary that the predications of the individuals (of the human species) may also differ.

There are persons who, rising above the rank of humanity, progress towards angelhood; they are completely diverted from the ugliness of this world. Then there are some persons who shunning humanity are moving towards bestiality and absolute ugliness, and are diverted from the angelic purity. In this case, it is necessary that the colour of both the sides (angelic and bestial) may be imprinted on the Holy Fold from where the administration of the Universal Soul proceeds towards its body. It is also necessary that their imprint on it may render the descending Divine Grace to get coloured with a colour which may slightly differ from the just and plain predication.

This is how the affair will continue ascending and descending until it becomes necessary in the wisdom of God, that the Destiny (*Qaḍā'*) may descend for the extinction of the species, nay, for the extinction of all the species of the animals and the vegetables. Then Destiny waits for the conjunction of the heavenly bodies and the earthly situation which require that extinction. When both the heavenly and the earthly causes are found requiring that extinction, then the coming of the Resurrection becomes necessary. This is the predication of the Universal Soul and of the order (*tartīb*) that calls for it.

Similarly, when the number of such individuals who are inclined to devilry and bestiality multiplies and there is no one to check their evil, it becomes necessary that Destiny should come down to the Holy Fold for raising a messenger and revealing a Book. Destiny then waits for the appearance of a person, pure of sin and most intelligent, who combines in his person such powers of the stars which may lead to his dominion, the establishment of his religion and guidance, and which also may become the cause of effecting unity among the people, and of the flow of different kinds of sciences from him. When that man is found, Destiny gushes out from his breast, and the Law and guidance are represented in a plane (*mauṭin*) just between the Unseen and the Seen.

For example, even though the matter of the Law (*Sharī'ah*) is the sayings and orders of the Holy Prophet, it is not what it actually is. How more approximately it resembles the intellectual form! When you think of a man you will have his form reflected on the tablet of your mind, but the form of the man is not the man himself. It is only his appearance. If you look at the form from the point of its being an accidental object and the one which subsists by your intellect, then that would be an object far removed from the reality of the man. But if you were to give such a look at it (form) which (look) penetrating it (form) reaches the reality of the man behind it, your attention will not end at the form of man but rather at his reality. The form would be just like a glass to which you will pay no attention whatsoever.

Similarly, though the Law (*Sharī'ah*) is included in the sayings and sciences of the Holy Prophet, it in one respect is outside them and in the other respect is connected with them. We, however, do not give decision about it and say that it is the result of the Divine Manifestation (*Tajallī*) or is the outcome of the revelation of that reality which is named as the prophet of the prophets, but can say so in some other respect. It is, therefore, your duty to contemplate.[1]

In short, this order is as carefully looked after in the body of the Universal Soul as that administration is carefully looked after, which, flowing from the species, penetrates its individuals with the result that nothing takes place in the world but according to it.

As regards the life-account of the Holy Prophet in connection with his habits, qualities and his beauty, it all has a recourse to his having been created in the best form, and having been blessed and supported by the Holy Fold. It is, therefore, that he is distinguished in many of these qualities from other human beings.

These are the last words which we intended to bring into this

1. Here Shāh Ṣāḥib seems to effect an agreement between the orthodox view and the one held by others like Ibn Masarrah and Rāzī, that prophecy is a philosophic sanctification and a purifiying illumination, which is the result of an ascetic rapture. See *Saṭa'āt*, Saṭ' 22, where Shāh Walīyullāh states that the revelation of the Qur'ān is the result of the perfection of the self (*nafs*) of the Prophet and of the fulfilment of the rights on the part of the Great Manifestation (*Tajallī-A'ẓam*).

treatise. All praise is due to God, the Lord of the worlds. God is enough for me and He is the best protector. May God send His blessings upon our chief Muhammad, upon his family and upon his Companions.

INDEX